Discovering C

A guide for those who like to see for themselves

Jon Grant

First edition published in December 2017 by jgrantbooks

E mail:jgrantbooks@virginmedia.com

Note. The material contained in this book is set out in good faith for general guidance and no liability can be accepted for loss or expense incurred as a result of relying in particular circumstances on statements made in the book.

ISBN: 978-1-9999201-0-4

Printed and bound by CPI Group (UK) Ltd, Croydon, CRO 4YY

Front cover: Tower Bridge

Back cover: Royal Hospital for Seamen, Greenwich

Contents

Preface

I commuted to London for about 40 years but never really understood its history or explored my surroundings. Retirement has given be the opportunity to rectify this and to enjoy visiting London's many magnificent historical sites. I wish I had researched the city sooner and thereby better appreciated my urban environment. I hope that this book will help others to avoid making the same mistake and, in a very small way, that their lives will therefore be enriched.

Discovering Old London has three main sections:

1. Introductory chapters, largely based on royal dynasties, provide the historical context; added detail is given in the Detailed notes section at the end of the book. These chapters contain both a Timeline and a listing of suggested London 'Top spots' that relate to each of the periods (those 'Top spots' that I think really should not be missed have been marked as **ESSENTIAL**).

2. An index of the 'Top spots', organised by London post code, and

3. A Glossary of terms, including architectural terms, many of which I have illustrated. The first use of a term has been highlighted in the opening chapters by the use of *italics*.

Unsurprisingly most of the main sites are buildings and architecture is therefore one of the main themes of the book. Tracking the different styles of architecture can be difficult as many of the more important London buildings have been reconstructed or significantly modified over time. Because **Discovering Old London** has been organised on a chronological basis, it will be necessary to refer to a number of chapters to fully understand the evolution of buildings such as Lambeth Palace or Westminster Abbey. Hopefully this will be facilitated by the index which is embedded in the listing of 'Top spots' organised by post code.

About a half of these 'Top spots' are in what today is known as the 'City', the financial area that is governed by the Corporation of London. In the text I have used a capital 'C' sparingly and most references to the metropolis are to the 'city'. I hope this does not cause either confusion or irritation.

My wife, Lesley, and sons, Nick and Chris, have been very supportive and offered good advice and encouragement. So too have a number of friends and particular thanks go to Robert Woolf who has been generous in sharing his considerable knowledge of London with me and Rick Browning who is the master of all things related to presentation and technology. Catherine Bradley, David Parry, Henry Staunton and David White have been kind enough to read drafts and make very helpful suggestions for improvement. My thanks also go to Tony Heal of Chipstead Services for his patience when photocopying numerous copies of drafts of the book and to Kelly Brown of CPI for printing the final version.

While I have benefited from much assistance any faults in this book are my own and I apologise for them. I can imagine that some will think that I have over simplified and omitted relevant information. This may well be true. History is very complicated and here is inevitably much more that could be written, indeed there are several much more comprehensive books on London but they are 'long reads'. I have tried to be concise and structure the information to make it easily accessible for busy people. My aim has been to sketch an overview and hopefully encourage the young, their parents and, like me, the retired to discover Old London for themselves.

Jon Grant   **December 2017**

Introduction

London is soon to have its 2,000th birthday. This book summarises the history of this great city from its first creation by the Romans up to the beginning of the twentieth century and describes what can be seen today from the different historical periods. Most of these remains are buildings and the changing styles of architecture are dealt with in each chapter. Other recurring themes are the rate of growth of London's population, the importance of London's port to its growth and prosperity and the regeneration that took place following periodic disasters.

Growth in London's population

It is thought that London's population in Roman times might have been around 30,000 but this declined rapidly after the Romans left and did not reach that level again until around 1200. The city's population then grew until the Black Death, a catastrophe from which it took over a century to recover from. Commencing in the Tudor period, London's population expanded at a rate faster than the rest of the country. In the Georgian, Regency and Victorian periods the rate of growth was simply staggering.

While this population increase was linked to rural depopulation and latterly to reductions in the death rate, foreign immigration also played an important role. London was a 'melting pot' that seemed to attract the dispossessed of Europe like a magnet. At different times, Jews, Dutch and French Huguenots and Irish came in large numbers. This brought new ideas, raw energy and ambition to London. It is hard to believe for example that the massive Victorian construction projects would have been possible without the manual labour provided by the Irish or that the City's financial service industry would have evolved to be so significant without the various contributions of Italians, Jews and Dutch.

1

	Estimated London population	Proportion of England's population
1100	15,000	1%
1200	30,000	1%
1300	80,000	1%
1400	35,000	1%
1500	60,000	2%
1600	250,000	6%
1700	600,000	12%
1800	1,000,000	12%
1850	2,700,000	18%
1900	6,700,000	22%

Additional people, of course, needed accommodation and the expansion of London's footprint is closely linked to the demographics. London remained largely within its old boundaries until 1600 and thereafter expanded in all directions. Not surprisingly, the largest increase in area was in the nineteenth century but, as shown below, even by 1900, the area of Victorian London was only about half of today's Greater London.

Introduction

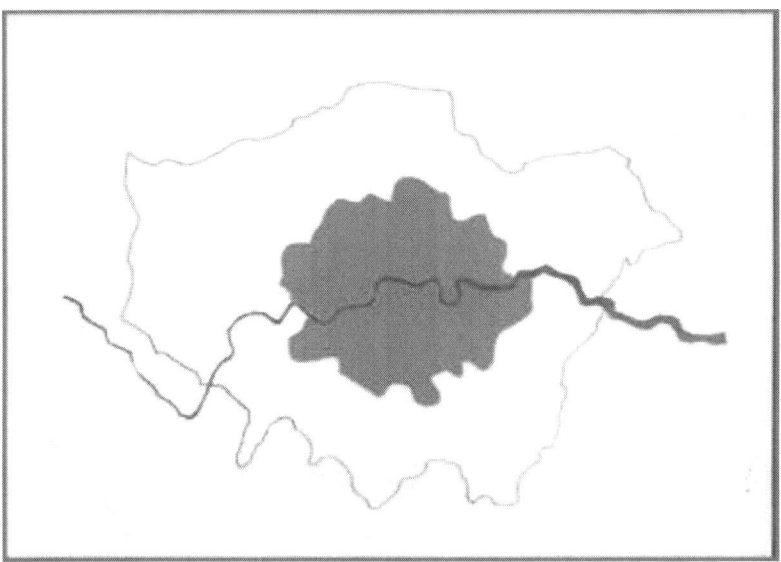

London around 1900 (shaded) with the boundary of today's Greater London

Importance of London's port

The early years of Roman occupation necessitated imported supplies to support the army and London, blessed as it was with proximity to Gaul and located on a deep tidal river, met the invaders' needs for a port. The wall that was built to protect the Roman city around the year 200 provided protection for the next 1300 years and helped London to establish itself as England's main trading centre. In Tudor times most of the country's wool exports passed through the city as well as many of its imports. Much of this trade was with our close neighbours in Continental Europe.

The city was well placed to benefit from the expansion of international trade in the Tudor, Stuart and especially the Georgian periods. Much of

3

this trade was long distance especially with the new colonies in America, India and the West Indies. International trade generated wealth and skills and capitalistic avarice drove the desire for more of both. By 1820, with its modern docks and with the expertise in ship broking, insurance and banking services that collectively provide the necessary infrastructure for trade, London was well placed to benefit from the country's Industrial Revolution and its expanding Empire. The rest, as they say, 'is history'!

The periodic need for regeneration

Fire was inevitably a constant threat to a large population living close together in houses that, for most of London's existence, were made of wood. Within a few years of its establishment the city was torched by Boudicca and fire was to reap havoc on many occasions before the 1666 inferno. The Great Fire was a catalyst for rebuilding the city in stone but this did not bring an end to the problem and serious fires continued into the Victorian period. While the fires would have caused great personal hardship, reconstruction gave architects the opportunity for creativity. Some of London's finest buildings such as the Palace of Westminster, the Royal Exchange, St Paul's Cathedral and about 20 Wren churches are, in effect, phoenixes rising from the ashes.

In the twentieth century bombs, first German and then Irish, destroyed many buildings although it is to the credit of the authorities that so much has been salvaged. The twenty-first century will, no doubt, bring new challenges and, in the distance, there is the possibility that rising sea levels resulting from climate change will drown much of the city. Humans are extremely resourceful but there can be no certainty that all of our architectural heritage while be saved. Enjoy it while you can!

Pre-history

Overview

Historically the Thames was wider and shallower than today. Although the Thames' tidal head has varied over time, for many years it was about where Central London now is. This, and a series of islands on the south bank, would have eased the challenges of Ancient Britons wanting to cross the river. The Thames was an important means of transport, source of food and almost certainly had religious significance. Although only relatively few signs of human activity prior to the Romans have been discovered, it is hard to believe that the London area was not well used in pre-historical times. Much more evidence is probably buried below the layers of settlement of the last two thousand years.

The Ice Ages and the Interglacial periods of the Palaeolithic Age

The Palaeolithic (or 'old' stone age) lasted almost a million years. The climate changed several times in this period with at least three 'Ice Ages' and, between them, warmer 'Interglacials'. Although the ice never reached the south east of England, the area was often too cold for human habitation. In the Interglacials nomadic hunter-gathers would visit and some of the oldest bone fragments, which date back around 400,000 years, have been found close to the Thames at Swanscombe, Kent. These fragments of the skull of an early Neanderthal woman are on display at the Natural History Museum.

About 800,000 years ago the Thames was a tributary of the massive Bytham River that flowed east before it joined the Rhine and from there flowed north creating the flood plain that is now covered by the North

Sea. The ice sheet created during the Anglian Glacial around 480,000 years ago covered the Bytham and shifted the Thames about ten miles south into its current valley.

Changes in sea level caused by subsequent cold and warm periods caused the Thames to flow at different speeds and there were alternating periods of rapid erosion and the deposition of glacial debris that created the four gravel terraces that underlie much of Central London. Two of these terraces can be traced in the contours around Trafalgar Square. The higher, earlier, terrace is about 400,000 to 300,000 years old and flint axes have been found in it that would have been used by early man to butcher animals. The lower terrace dates to around 110,000 years ago when, despite being warmer than today, Britain was unpopulated. Not surprisingly this layer of gravel contains no flint tools, but does contain animal bones including those of lions and hippopotami. In later years the low hills formed from this gravel were to be one of the factors making London so suitable for settlement by the Romans.

Little evidence of occupation from the Mesolithic Age

Around 9,500 BC the climate warmed and Britain entered the current Interglacial, the Holocene. Tundra was replaced by grassland and gradually animal life returned. Homo Sapiens hunter-gatherers entered South East 'England' across the land bridge with the Continent. These Mesolithic (or 'middle' stone age) people were nomadic and there is little evidence of their existence near the Thames other than a few antler harpoon tips that have been found at Battersea and Wandsworth.

Some evidence of occupation during the Neolithic Age

A period of rapid transformation commenced around 4,500 BC that is called the Neolithic (or 'new' stone) Age. Immigrants from Continental Europe brought with them knowledge of both pastoral and arable farming as well as domesticated livestock and new strains of grain. Forests were cleared and farming replaced hunter-gathering as the primary source of food. Permanent settlements were established, pottery was introduced and a new tradition involving the construction of earthworks and giant stone 'megalithic' monuments commenced.

The Thames Basin is likely to have been amongst the first areas to be settled by people from the Continent but the area is not rich in evidence of Neolithic occupation. Remains of a *causewayed enclosure* have been found at Yeoveney Lodge near Staines dating to about 3,500 BC and one of the oldest *long barrows* is at Coldrum in Kent. The water is a richer source of evidence of the Neolithic period as the Thames likely had religious significance and *votive offerings* were made in it. In particular, a number of polished stone axe heads have been found at Mortlake, Hammersmith and Fulham. These would have been highly valued symbols of power as several were made of stone from as far away as Orkney and Cumbia. Many axe heads are on display in the Museum of London.

...more evidence of Bronze Age man

The advent of metal, first copper and then bronze, around 2,500 BC was to significantly change the lives and culture of Ancient Britons. While metal artefacts were more functional than those made from wood and stone they also had status value and became a method of exchanging and storing wealth. Control over the production of, and trade in, metal tools and weapons gave a relatively small number of individuals the means to increase their power and authority. As the period progressed, society became more hierarchical and materialistic.

The Thames was obviously important to Bronze Age people and votive offerings continued to be made. The Dagenham Idol,[1] the Battersea Shield and many bronze spear heads and swords have been found in the river. At Vauxhall remains of wooden posts dating to around 1600 BC can be seen at very low tide. These are thought to relate to a wooden causeway built to give access to an island that marked the tidal head[2] at that time and would therefore have had special significance. A Bronze Age cemetery has been found at Hayes and near Beckton there are remains of a wooden trackway from this period possibly used for herding cattle across a marshy area.

...and of Iron Age Celts

Starting around 800 BC the Iron Age was another period of significant technological change originating from the Continent. As with the Bronze Age, this may have involved widespread immigration or the transfer of the new skills and ideas to the existing population by a relatively small number of newcomers. As well as the gradual replacement of bronze tools and weapons by iron ones, farming techniques improved and, in particular, the introduction of iron-tipped ploughshares allowed the cultivation of the heavy clay soils found in valleys. Initially Iron Age people, later called *Celts*, lived in hill forts but as the period progressed larger settlements were built in the valleys.

The Thames formed the border between two Celtic tribes and it is therefore perhaps not surprising that Julius Caesar makes no mention of any large Celtic settlements in the London area when he invaded in 55 BC and again the following year. There is however an Iron Age hill fort on Wimbledon Common (now called 'Caesar's Camp') and larger

Pre-history

enclosed sites at Uphall Camp, Ilford, and at Woolwich Arsenal.[3] There may also have been a major centre west of London, possibly in the Barn Elms/Putney area, perhaps guarding an important crossing point of the Thames. Votive offerings continue to have been deposited in the river and the Waterloo Helmet and Wandsworth Shield, with their impressive *La Tene* motifs, are on display in the British Museum

Roman London

Overview of the period between 43 and 410

For a period of just under four hundred years Britannia, as it came to be known, was a small province on the north-western periphery of the Roman Empire. While not all local traditions were to be lost, Britain was significantly changed by an influx of people from all corners of the Roman Empire, by the creation of cities and by the operation of an extensive bureaucratic and legal regime using Latin as the official language. The population grew and elite Romano-Britons became wealthy and succumbed to the comforts of the Roman way of life. However, as the powers of Rome waned the economy deteriorated and when the army withdrew, Britain found it impossible to protect itself from its bellicose neighbours.

London, or rather Londinium, rapidly grew to be Roman Britain's dominant city. At the height of its importance around 150, it had a population of perhaps 30,000 inhabitants and was the country's administrative centre and major port. While remaining a major Roman city its relative importance reduced after about 200. The city was probably abandoned soon after the Roman administration ended in 410.

Londinium first established

Established within the first few years of Claudius' invasion in 43, Londinium protected the north bank of the crossing point of the Thames on the route between the important settlements of Dover, Canterbury and Rochester to the south and Colchester and St. Albans to the north. The Roman city was centred on the River Walbrook and the low hills at

Ludgate and Cornhill that lay on either side of it. Because of the underlying gravel, the forest was relatively light and easily cleared and the ground was well drained.

The Thames was much wider then than today. At low tide, it was about 300 yards across and at high tide perhaps a thousand yards. Due to islands on the south bank, the Thames at Londinium was narrow enough for crossing but still deep enough to be accessed by seagoing ships. Its placement at the Thames' tidal head facilitated the construction of a bridge and this became the focal point for the road system.[4] It is thought that initially a wooden pontoon bridge was built which, around 85, was upgraded to a bridge supported by wooden piles and with a central drawbridge.

As is evidenced by a layer of red ash that lies below the old city, Londinium was completely destroyed by fire during Boudicca's rebellion of 60. However, within a decade, the city had been rebuilt by the military as a planned Roman town and it grew rapidly. The waterfront was reconstructed to have sturdy wooden wharves and large warehouses and a forum, temples and baths[5] were built in stone. A large building discovered near Cannon Street station is believed to have been the Governor's residence (or praetorium) complete with a garden, pools, and several large halls. Around 90 a massive *basilica* was located on the northern edge of the forum near to the intersection of the present Gracechurch, Lombard, and Fenchurch Streets. About the year 122 a fort was constructed at Cripplegate large enough to accommodate a thousand troops.

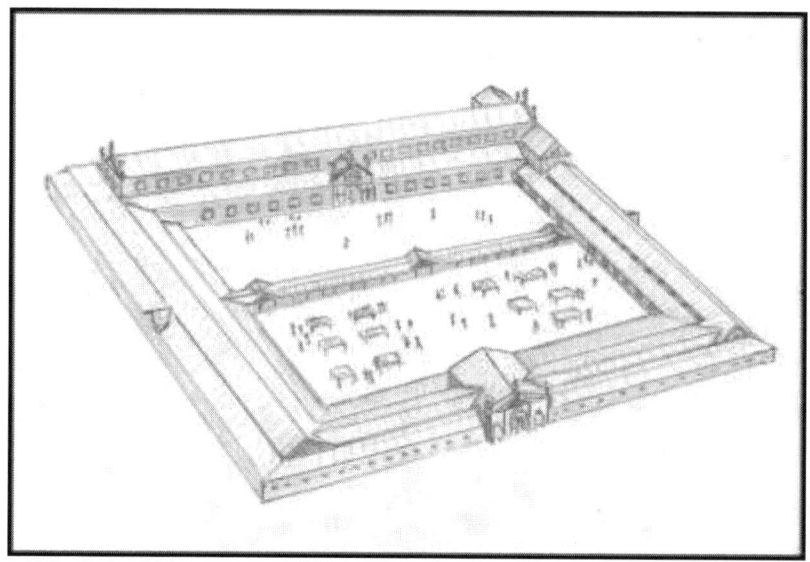

Model of Forum and Basilica in the Museum of London

There was also Roman activity south of the river in Southwark and Borough. From an early date houses lined Watling Street and Stane Street before they met to cross the bridge and remains of substantial Roman buildings have been discovered under both Southwark Cathedral and Winchester Palace.

Londinium at its peak

Londinium was at its peak between 150 and 200. It had replaced Colchester in importance and had a population of perhaps 30,000 inhabitants. After a large fire in 125 many public buildings had been rebuilt and a stone amphitheatre was erected in the area that is now largely under the yard outside Guildhall. The town had piped water and a sophisticated drainage system. The river bank was not in its current location but over a hundred yards inland, just north of present day Thames Street. Falling sea levels and silting meant that over time new quays had to be constructed that increasingly encroached into the river.

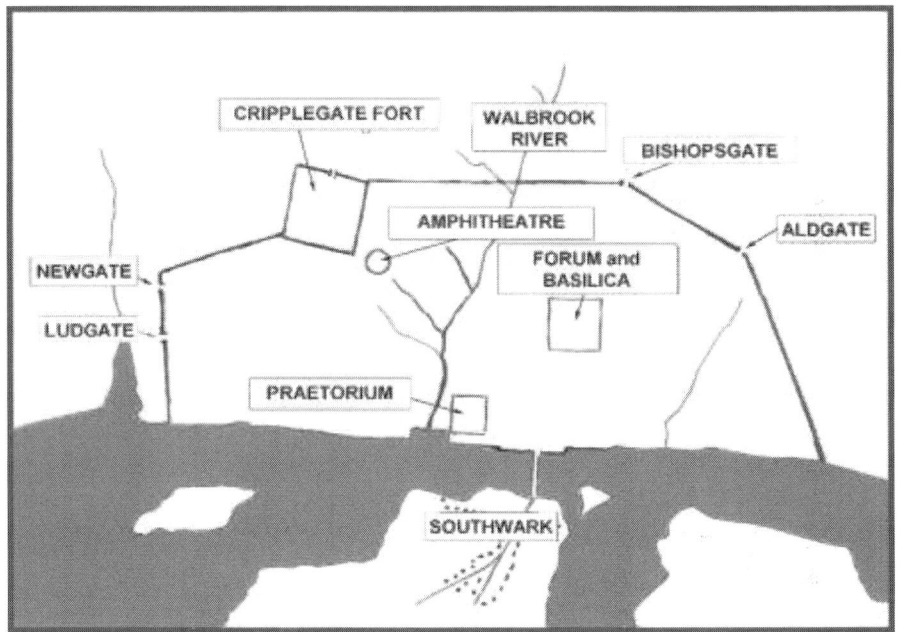

Outline of Roman London around 200

Around 200 the Romans built a defensive wall (the hugh amount of Kentish ragstone for which was quarried near Maidstone) around the landward side of the city. The wall was originally about two miles long, six yards high and two yards thick. Five gates[6] (clockwise from the west: Ludgate, Newgate, Cripplegate, Bishopsgate and Aldgate) were aligned to the network of Roman roads radiating out of the city. The north-western corner of the wall incorporated the fort at Cripplegate, but the fort's walls had to be strengthened and heighted. In the next century the wall was extended alongside the Thames[7] and semi-circular bastion towers were built on the eastern part of the landward wall. The settlement south of the river remained unfortified.

Londinium in decline

Londinium's fortunes were to wane after 150 and its population probably fell. The cause for this is uncertain but disease is a possibility as the Antonine Plague decimated populations in other parts of western Europe between 165 and 190. York became increasingly important, especially after Roman Britain was divided into two for administrative purposes in 216. Around 300 Britain was split into four administrative units and Lincoln and Cirencester grew in relative importance. There was also reduced commercial activity in the south east. Trade with the Continent was adversely affected by chaos in Gaul and, with most of the army stationed around Hadrian's Wall, military supplies were largely imported through northern ports.

After a rebellion in 285, in which Carausius seized control of Britain for seven years, it appears that Londinium's basilica and forum were demolished (perhaps as a punishment to the city for the support it provided to the rebels). Further crises were to follow as Roman Britain came under increasing pressure from barbarian attack and periodic conspiracies destabilised the army and subverted the central authority of Rome.

From 313 Christianity was tolerated in the Roman Empire (although it did not become the official religion until 391) and it seems likely that a Christian cathedral[8] was built in Londinium. This apart there was little new building in the 300s and the amphitheatre was allowed to become derelict and the Temple of Mithras was abandoned. Around 368 Londinium was renamed 'Augusta'. In 410 the Roman army withdrew and Britain ceased to be a Roman province. Public services ceased and the economy rapidly deteriorated. It is generally thought that within a generation the British had reverted to their rural Celtic ways and Londinium had been abandoned as the buildings became unsafe.

Timeline

	National events	London events
43	Claudius invades Britain	
50		Londinium established
59		First bridge constructed
60	Boudicca's rebellion	City razed to the ground
70		Forum, baths and temples built
85		Wooden pile bridge constructed
90		Basilica built
122	Hadrian's Wall built	
130		Stone amphitheatre built
200		London Wall constructed
216	Roman Britain subdivided	
285	Carausian Rebellion	Basilica and forum demolished
313	Christianity tolerated	
367	Britain attacked by Scots, Picts and Saxons	
410	Roman administration ends	

Top spots

All Hallows-by-the-Tower, EC3	The church was built on the site of a former Roman building. The crypt museum contains the tessellated floor of a domestic house as well as a fine model of Roman London.
London Mithraeum Bloomberg, EC4	The Temple of Mithras was built on the bank of the Walbrook around 220 and was abandoned in the fourth century. The Mithraeum provides what is described as 'an immersive experience' of the ancient temple together with a selection of the Roman artefacts found during recent excavations.
Museum of London, EC2 **ESSENTIAL**	The museum holds many of the Roman artefacts found during excavations. There are also some splendid models of the Upper Thames Street baths, the Roman bridge, the forum and Roman houses.
Roman Amphitheatre, EC2	Around 70 the Romans built a wooden amphitheatre, which was rebuilt in stone in the early second century. About a third of the amphitheatre has been excavated and can be accessed through Guildhall Art Gallery. A ring of black paving stones in Guildhall Yard shows its full extent.
Roman Wall, Tower Hill, EC3	The only remaining part of the Roman wall stands just to the east of the Tower Hill underground station, elsewhere. the remains are medieval. At Tower Hill the bottom half of the wall, built of ragstone with horizontal courses of red clay tiles, is Roman.

Early Medieval London

Overview of the period between 410 and 1154

The Early Medieval period involved the Romano-British and Celtic communities being dominated by, in succession, Saxons, Vikings and Normans. While the collapse of Roman Britain saw a gradual decline in living standards, the country was still wealthy and relatively under-populated and this acted as a magnet for Saxon immigrants. Over time four main Saxon kingdoms evolved (East Anglia, Northumberland, Mercia and Wessex) and three minor ones (Essex, Kent and Sussex). The story of Saxon Britain is of competition between these kingdoms against a backdrop of gradual economic development and the resurgence of Christianity. Londinium was probably abandoned soon after the Roman army withdrew from Britain and its regeneration was slow. Within about 200 years a small Saxon trading settlement known as Lundenwic had been established west of the old Roman city walls. Lundenwic flourished and inevitably became a target for Viking invaders.

At the end of the eighth century the Vikings started to pillage much of Western Europe. England's unprotected east coast and wealthy monasteries proved an irresistible target. Initial raiding was to lead to a full invasion and, by 874, all but Wessex was occupied. Led by Alfred the Great, the Viking advance was stopped and, around 886, the Saxons created Lundenburg within the old Roman city walls. Wessex prevailed and England was first partitioned and eventually unified. A period of economic growth resulted but the Vikings were to return and the Danish Canute ruled England for over 20 years. For a short period the country returned to Saxon rule under Edward the Confessor and, around 1042, he commenced building an abbey and a palace in the area we now call

17

Westminster. However, the Vikings (this time the French branch known as the Normans) were to return in 1066.

Much of the Anglo-Saxon ruling hierarchy died at the Battle of Hastings and those nobles who survived quickly lost their rights and land to the invaders. A new Norman culture, with its different language and customs, was rapidly imposed. However, both London and the separate Westminster remained important centres of power and, by 1154, London was again England's largest and most important city.

Saxon Lundenwic to the west of the old city

After the Romans quit Britain in 410 the infrastructure they had created soon collapsed and the importance of cities, including Londinium, rapidly diminished. During the next century, Saxon[9] invaders gained power but they were subsistence farmers rather than city dwellers and initially trade was very limited. Londinium was abandoned[10] and its buildings and river wharves fell into disrepair.

By 640, a Saxon trading settlement (or 'wic') had been established west of the Roman city walls around the area that is now Covent Garden. Lundenwic, as the area become known, was initially part of the Kingdom of the East Saxons and, by 670, it had grown into a thriving commercial centre. Saxon traders used the river bank along today's Strand (the word meant 'beach') to load and unload shallow-draft boats. Trade in wool and cloth was especially important. Wool was transported to the wic by river from the Cotswolds for export and woven cloth was imported from Gaul and the Low Countries.

Around 730 the Saxon Mercian kings became dominant and took control of the city. St. Alban's Church, Wood Street is said to have been built on the site of the Chapel Royal of King Offa. Wharves were constructed along the Thames and the first monastery was built on Thorney (an island formed by rivulets of the River Tyburn) at what is today called Westminster. However, within a hundred years life in Ludenwic was to be disrupted by the Vikings. Trade with the continent lessened because of Viking piracy and there were direct Viking attacks on the city in 842 and 851. Ludenwic was eventually occupied by the Vikings after Britain was invaded by the 'Great Heathen Army' in 865.

Saxon Lundenburg within the Roman city walls

The Saxon kingdom of Wessex resisted and, after years of conflict, Alfred the Great forced the Viking leaders to sue for peace. In 886 Alfred re-established a town, Lundenburg, within the defences provided by the old Roman city walls, as one of a number of defensive *burghs* created around the country. The need for the security provided by the Roman walls meant that Lundenwic was abandoned, although the name still survives as Aldwych (or the 'old wic'). Trade prospered, coins were minted and a new street system emerged. Through the 920s, the city became the most important commercial centre in England with eight mints as well as new wharves and markets. During the late Saxon times many churches were built, funded by the generosity of rich merchants. South of the river, another burgh was established by Alfred at Southwark, (the name is thought to mean 'the defensive work of the men of Surrey') and a King's Manor was established.

Viking raids returned in 982 and 994 and measures were taken to protect the city including the construction of a low wooden bridge to prevent Viking longboats passing upstream.[11] Lundenberg remained outside Danish control until 1013 when it was captured by Sweyn

Forkbeard and his son Canute. When both Sweyn and his Saxon opponent Edmund died Canute became king and ruled from Westminster. For thirty years trade flourished around a Viking community possibly living outside the walls near the church of St. Clement Danes.

In 1042, Canute's step-son, the Saxon King Edward the Confessor, was crowned. The pious Edward is remembered for building a palace and the important Benedictine abbey at Westminster. The east end of the abbey was completed just in time for Edward to be buried there in 1066; the rest of the building was not completed until 1080. The enormous arcaded abbey church was designed by Norman architects and became known as the 'west minster' to distinguish it from St. Paul's Cathedral (the 'east minster'). Little remains today of either Edward's abbey or his palace but these sites, and the buildings on them, have had great significance over the following millennium.

Norman control

Following the Battle of Hastings, William the Conqueror recognised the strategic importance of London[12] and the need to harness the support of its population. Initially London resisted but it surrendered after Southwark was torched. As an act of reconciliation William soon confirmed that the city's laws and customs would continue to apply. Indeed, the city's powers were to grow under Henry I and Stephen as London was granted the right to collect taxes and select its own sheriffs (the representatives of royal authority). The City of London became a recognisable institution.

Despite these accommodations the Normans maintained a strong military presence. William I constructed the White Tower (part of what today is known as the Tower of London) in the east and Montfichet's

Tower and Baynard's Castle[13] near Ludgate Hill in the west. Windsor Castle was also built less than a day's march to the west. Norman monarchs moved around the country and Winchester, Gloucester and York were other important locations for them. However, the Palace of Westminster was the prime royal residence throughout the Norman period, and the court was based in Westminster attracting merchants and workshops to the area. William II built Westminster Hall in 1097 and courtiers and churchmen built town houses (or 'inns') along the Strand, the main highway between Westminster and London.

The Norman kings harnessed the power of the church to assist their colonisation of the country. Imposing cathedrals were built in Canterbury, Durham, Ely and Winchester and, in London, the new Westminster Abbey and St. Paul's Cathedral (largely reconstructed after having been destroyed by fire in 1087) were amongst the largest churches in Europe. A number of monasteries and hospitals were also established especially in Clerkenwell (where, as its name suggests, there was a good supply of fresh water) and Southwark. The twelfth century was also a time when many churches were built and, by 1183, there were more than a hundred of them within the city walls. While little remains of these churches today, later churches were generally built on the same sites and the structure of the parishes and the City of London's administrative system[14] endures.

Timeline

	National events	London events
449	Saxon mercenaries land in Kent	Londinium largely deserted
640		Lundenwic evolves
730		First monastery at Westminster
865	Viking invasion	
886		Lundenburg created within the Roman walls
899	Death of King Alfred	
1000		Wooden London Bridge built
1042		Building of a Palace and Abbey at Westminster commenced
1066	Norman invasion	
1078		Building of the White Tower commenced
1087	William II crowned	
1097		Construction of Westminster Hall commenced
1100	Henry I crowned	
1123		St Bartholomew's Priory founded in Smithfield
1135	Stephen crowned	
1154	Death of Stephen brings an end to the Norman dynasty	

Early medieval architecture

Early medieval architecture is known as 'Romanesque', so called because of the influence of the buildings of Ancient Rome. Romanesque buildings are known for their thick walls, round arches, sturdy pillars, *barrel vaults*, simple *capitals* and decorative *blank arcading*. All the weight of the roof was taken by the walls and, because of this, *buttresses* were often needed and windows were small and interiors dark. The introduction of *groin vaulting* strengthened buildings as some of the weight of the roof was taken by supporting piers thereby relieving some of the pressure from the walls.

Remaining evidence of Saxon architecture in London is sparse. Saxon buildings were seldom built of stone and, when they were, they have usually been replaced or destroyed by fire. There is more to see from Norman times when stone was used for churches and castles. The church of St. Bartholomew-the-Great and the Chapel of St. John in the Tower of London are good examples of the imposing Norman Romanesque style with thick columns, simple barrel and groin vaulting and rounded window openings. Towards the end of the period it was discovered that it was stronger to build the groins as separate arches (or ribs) and *rib vaulting* started to be used.

Chapel of St. John in the Tower of London

Top spots

All Hallows-by-the-Tower, EC3	This ancient church contains a seventh-century Saxon Romanesque arch built from discarded Roman tiles. In the *crypt*, the Chapel of St Francis of Assisi, although dating from 1280, is a good example of Romanesque barrel vaulting.
Palace of Westminster, SW1	Westminster Hall was one of the largest Norman Romanesque style halls in Europe. However, the hall was modified in the Late Medieval period and only the walls of the original Norman hall remain.
St. Bartholomew-the-Great, EC1 **ESSENTIAL**	Originally part of an Augustinian Priory founded in 1123, much of the priory's church was demolished in 1543 during the Dissolution of the Monasteries. However, the original galleried *choir* remains with its fine Norman Romanesque columns and vaulted aisles. The *crossing* has both round and pointed arches (the earliest example of the use of pointed arches in London).
St. Mary-le-Bow, EC2	The impressive Norman crypt remains as a restaurant. Its arches (or 'bows') possibly gives the name to the church which was rebuilt by Wren after the Great Fire.
Temple Church, EC4	The circular nave has a Norman exterior and a highly decorated west doorway. Inside there is extensive round-arch arcading.

Tower of London, EC3 **ESSENTIAL**	The White Tower replaced the original wooden structure built soon after 1066. Completed in 1098, the tower was intended to be a royal residence as well as a stronghold. Fireplaces provided warmth and latrines were built into the walls. On the second floor is the impressive early Norman Romanesque Chapel of St. John with its thick round columns with capitals with simple carvings of scallop and leaf designs.
Westminster Abbey, SW1	Some evidence of the Saxon Romanesque abbey can be seen in the columns of the cloisters and the *undercroft*. The Norman Pyx Chamber with its groin vaulting, rounded arches and massive central column is thought to be the oldest standing building in London.

Late Medieval London

Overview of the period between 1154 and 1485

Peace in the civil war between the last Norman king Stephen and his cousin Matilda was only achieved by Stephen accepting Matilda's son as his heir. This resulted in another family, the Plantagenets, holding the English throne for the three centuries that were the Late Middle Ages. The new king, Henry II, was Duke of Anjou and his marriage to Eleanor of Aquitaine gave him even more territory in France. This period saw almost continual war in France as the Plantagenets lost, regained and lost again their territory there. In order to obtain financial and military support for this fighting the kings were forced to obtain the support of the English nobility and this resulted in constraints to royal power. By the end of the Late Middle Ages, English monarchs had defined duties to the realm that were underpinned by a sophisticated justice system.

The first half of the Late Middle Ages benefitted from the long reigns and strong leadership of Henry II, Edward I and Edward III. There was economic growth and the English gained control over Scotland and Wales. The magnificent Decorated Gothic architectural style evolved and in Westminster Abbey, the 'Old' St. Paul's Cathedral and the St. Stephen's Chapel, London had three of the finest ecclesiastical buildings in Europe.

The Black Death of 1348, which was broadly the mid-point of the Late Middle Ages, had a devastating impact. Half the population was killed and the plague was to return on a number of occasions. After Edward III there was a succession of relatively weak kings, the throne was usurped on three occasions and the country was beset with social and economic problems. In the aftermath of the loss of the French

27

territories, rivalry between Edward III's offspring brought about the bloody Wars of the Roses that culminated in the death of Richard III at the Battle of Bosworth Field. With it Plantagenet rule came to an end.

Although London's population fell as a result of the Black Death, business appears to have continued to flourish. Foreign trade expanded, London's priories and hospitals benefitted from endowments from wealthy merchants and its guilds strove to maximise profits. Henry III's splendid Palace of Westminster was the focal point for royalty and, from the mid-fifteenth century onwards, for Parliament.

Centralisation of government

The Palace of Westminster remained the centre of royal power during the Late Medieval period and an increasing number of departments of government, including the Royal Courts of Law and the Exchequer, were located there. While Parliament was peripatetic for most of the Middle Ages, both Simon de Montfort's 'Parliament' of 1265 and Edward I's 'Model Parliament' met in Westminster Hall and during the reign of Edward IV the practice of Parliament meeting in Westminster became normal. In 1340 land between London and Westminster, previously occupied by the Knights Templar, was leased to lawyers and the names Inner and Middle Temple survive until today.

London benefitted from its proximity to royal power although the relationship between the city and the Plantagenet kings was often turbulent. London's support for the Crown was always conditional on the monarch maintaining sufficient order for business and trade to flourish. Several Plantagenet kings failed to achieve this. London sided with the barons in forcing King John to sign the Magna Carta[15] in 1215 and played a role in both Simon de Montfort's rebellion of 1265 and the overthrow of Edward II in 1326. The Plantagenets needed London's wealth and were justifiably afraid of its mob. Both Henry II and Richard I ceded powers to the City of London and under King John the aldermen of the wards were permitted to elect a mayor. The first mayor, Henry Fitz-Ailwin, served from 1189 to 1212 and in 1354 Edward III granted use of the title of Lord Mayor. The Lord Mayor of London was by now the second most powerful person in the country after the monarch.

Growth of trade and the guilds

During the Late Medieval period London became the trading centre for the south east of England which supplied the city with food and fuel and was also a market for goods manufactured in London and imported by its merchants. Foreign trade expanded, especially with the Low Countries and the Baltic area. Exports included cloth, wool, tin and pewter; imports included wine, spices, dyes and furs. To accommodate this growth in trade the wharves were extended,[16] purpose-built warehouses were constructed (the earliest on the land owned by the Hanseatic[17] merchants) and formal wholesale markets were established. Cheapside[18] was the main retail area, with perhaps 400 shops, and an embryonic financial community started when Edward I granted land in the city to goldsmiths from Lombardy. In 1327 the City of London acquired the Kings Manor in Southwark from the Crown.

Trade groups such as mercers, fishmongers and candlemakers clustered together and guilds were formed that became increasingly powerful. Londoners had to belong to a guild before they could set up a shop, take an apprentice or hold civic office. Guilds were also important social institutions collecting taxes, encouraging law and order and providing welfare support. They had a strong link to the church and many endowed *chantry chapels*. Over time the guilds evolved into Livery Companies which were corporations formed under Royal Charter with responsibility for training their respective trades. The Livery Companies became involved in politics and, in due course, they became part of the governance of the City of London and voted in mayoral and sheriff elections. Inevitably they bickered amongst themselves about their relative importance[19] and tried to surpass each other with the splendour of their halls. A main guildhall building, acting as a town hall where taxes were paid, was probably in existence from around 1200. The current Guildhall, built between 1411 and 1450, was a strong symbol to royalty of the importance of the City of London.

Movement within the city was improved when, between 1176 and 1209, the wooden bridge across the Thames was replaced by a stone version. This first stone London Bridge, designed by Peter of Colechurch, had 19 narrow arches and a drawbridge in the middle. The drawbridge allowed ships access to upstream quays, at least until it ceased working in 1475. However, the narrow arches restricted the flow of water and the rapids that resulted made it dangerous to travel through them in small boats. Slowing the flow of the river also led to the water freezing in cold winters (especially during the, so called, Little Ice Age of the seventeenth century) and 'Frost Fairs'[20] were sometimes held.

Upkeep of the bridge was funded by tolls and rents from the houses and shops that were built on it. There were however periods of time when the bridge was poorly maintained, especially in the reign of Henry III. Traffic jams were common as the houses and shops meant that the width of the carriageway was restricted to fourteen feet. Many preferred to cross the river in small boats and the Thames watermen were to have plenty of business through to the seventeenth century. The buildings on the bridge also acted as a conduit for fire. Within three years of its opening in 1212, a fire broke out in Southwark, crossed London Bridge, and was responsible for killing 3,000 people in the city.

Model of London Bridge in the Church of St. Magnus-the-Martyr

Monks, nuns, friars and knights

After a fire in 1087, reconstruction of the 'Old' St. Paul's was commenced but a further fire in 1136 disrupted the work and the new cathedral was not finally completed until 1240. During the prolonged period of construction, the style of architecture changed and this was reflected in its 450 feet tall Gothic spire and pointed arches. If St. Paul's Cathedral was the City's prestige symbol, Westminster Abbey was the Crown's. In competition, Henry III demolished the dilapidated Saxon Westminster Abbey in 1245 and started rebuilding it as the home of a new shrine to Edward the Confessor.[21] By the time of Henry III's death in 1272, only the east end and the Chapter House had been built. This Gothic masterpiece was finally completed around 1390 in the reign of Richard II. Rather ironically, much of the early funding for the work came from fines and dispossessions from the persecuted Jewish community.

There was more to the medieval church than just fine buildings. It had important social as well as religious responsibilities and, for the needy and infirm, it represented the only hope of relief. During the twelfth and thirteenth centuries several substantial new monasteries and *hospitals* were established in and around the city. These probably started as simple wooden buildings but with the benefit of funding from merchants they were transformed into fine stone complexes each with their own church. Other than St. Helen's at Bishopsgate, most of the monasteries were just outside the city walls in Clerkenwell (St. Bartholomew's Priory and Hospital, Charterhouse and St. Mary's), Spitalfields (St. Mary's Spital, Holywell Nunnery and St Mary Bethlem - which by 1403 had become a hospital for the insane known as 'Bedlam') and Southwark (St. Mary's Overie, St. Thomas' Hospital and Bermondsey Abbey). From about 1250 *friars*, a new type of religious order working within the community, also thrived. The Knights Templar[22] had a substantial property just to the west of London on the Thames and the Knights Hospitaller (also known as the Knights of St. John) were based at the Priory of St. John in Clerkenwell.

Bishops were expected to sit in Parliament and many of them built houses in London, the size of which depended on the wealth of their Diocese. For example, the Bishop of Ely, who came from a wealthy wool producing area, built a large palace just outside the city walls in what is today Hatton Garden; its crypt remains below the Church of St Etheldreda. The Bishops of Exeter, Bath and Wells, Carlisle and Durham had fine palaces on the riverfront south of the Strand, the Bishops of Canterbury resided in Lambeth and the Bishops of Winchester owned a palace and extensive land in Southwark.

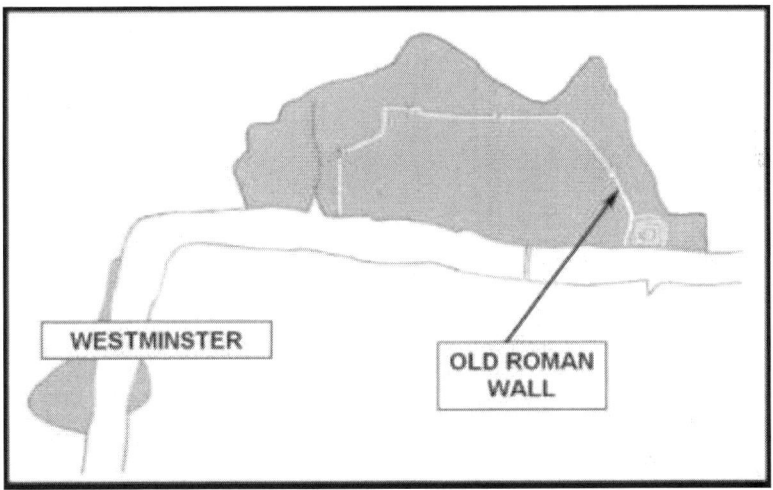

London around 1485

The church owned a third of the land within the city walls and this limited the space available for private dwellings. Increasingly there was building outside the walls and this led to a dispute with Westminster about the location of the administrative boundaries. This was resolved in 1222 with the size of the City of London being almost doubled to the present 'square mile'. The new City boundary was marked by posts, or 'bars'.

Pestilence and warfare

The size and importance of London led to the redevelopment of its defences. The city walls underwent substantial work especially in the reign of King John that included the addition of crenellations and further towers and bastions.[23] These walls provided protection against enemies but not disease. In 1348 London suffered badly from the Black Death epidemic[24] during which perhaps 40,000 Londoners died. There were at least three further outbreaks of the disease in the fourteenth century and another in 1407. Death rates were almost as high as in 1348. The population of London probably did not recover to pre-plague levels for about one hundred and fifty years.

Much of the sickness resulted from dirty water. Londoners relied on the Thames and its tributaries for their water supplies. In 1247 work began on building the Great Conduit, a lead pipe that brought water from a spring at Tyburn via Charing Cross, The Strand, Fleet Street and Ludgate to a large cistern in Cheapside. In the 1400s the system was extended to being about four miles in length in order to access springs at Paddington.

Not all the potential threats to the Plantagenet monarchs were from outside the walls. Evidence of civic unrest and the power of the mob can be seen from the progressive strengthening of the Tower of London in Late Medieval times. Richard I doubled its size and between 1230 and 1285 Henry III and his son, Edward I, encircled it with strong curtain walls and a broad moat (finally drained in 1843 after an outbreak of cholera) and ensured that the land entrance from the west was heavily defended. Not all the construction work was for defensive purposes and Henry III created a comfortable palace based on the St. Thomas, Wakefield and Lanthorn Towers and with a Great Hall in the In-most Ward (the area next to the White Tower).

This was the era of the Hundred Years' War (1337 - 1453) and the Wars of the Roses (1455 - 1485). Although the fighting in the Hundred Years' War was in France it had to be funded through increased taxation and this caused domestic unrest. In particular, the Peasants' Revolt in 1381 resulted in much damage in London including the burning of John of Gaunt's[25] Savoy Palace and the sacking of the Priory of St. John and Lambeth Palace. The revolt was concluded at Smithfield and the rioters were placated by promises made (but not kept) by a young Richard II.

Ultimately London turned against Richard and supported Henry Bolingbroke when he claimed the throne in 1399 as Henry IV. This led to the Wars of the Roses, a bloody conflict between the Houses of Lancaster and York. London was fortunate not to suffer much in this turbulent period although there was a short siege in 1471.[26] While broadly neutral, despite its initial support for Henry IV, London was more sympathetic to the House of York. Indeed, a number of London merchants were knighted in reward for supporting Edward IV when he grabbed the throne from Henry VI in 1461.

Timeline

	National events	London events
1154	Henry II, the first Plantagenet king, crowned	
1176		First stone London Bridge commenced
1189	Richard I crowned	The first Mayor of London appointed
1215	King John signs Magna Carta	
1216	Henry III crowned	
1222		City's boundaries extended
1230		Tower of London strengthened
1240		'Old' St. Paul's Cathedral completed
1245		Rebuilding of Westminster Abbey commenced
1265	Simon de Montfort's Parliament	
1272	Edward I crowned	
1292		St. Stephen's Chapel completed
1285		Tower of London further strengthened
1307	Edward II crowned	
1327	Edward III crowned	Edward II deposed

1337	Hundred Years' War commences	
1348	Black Death	40,000 Londoners died
1377	Richard II crowned	
1381	Peasants' Revolt	Wat Tyler killed at Smithfield
1397		Richard Whittington becomes mayor
1399	Henry IV, of the House of Lancaster, crowned	
1415	Henry V wins the Battle of Agincourt	
1422	Henry VI crowned	
1453	Hundred Years' War ends	
1455	Wars of the Roses commences	
1461	Edward IV, of the House of York, crowned	
1471		Battle of Barnet
1476		William Caxton establishes his first printing press at Westminster
1485	Death of Richard III and the end to the Wars of the Roses	

Late Medieval Gothic architecture

The Late Medieval period is most famous for its churches and public buildings built in the Gothic style with pointed arches, ribbed vaulting and *flying buttresses*. There were three phases: Early English Gothic (1200-1275), Decorated Gothic (1275-1350) and Perpendicular Gothic (1350-1530). The dates are approximate and some buildings are clearly transitional.

Model of 'Old' St. Paul's in the Museum of London

The most famous feature of Early English Gothic architecture is the replacement of rounded arches in windows and arcading by pointed ones. These arches were stronger because the blocks at the top of the arch press against each other rather than downwards. The chancel in Temple Church, the crossing in St. Bartholomew-the-Great and the crypt

38

to the Priory Church of St. John provide early examples of the use of pointed arches and therefore of the transition from Norman Romanesque.

However, the real revolution of Gothic architecture was the use of rib vaulting to create a skeleton to take more of the weight of the roof away from the walls. Early vaulting can be seen in the chancel in Temple Church (albeit restored after the Blitz), in the crypts of Guildhall, in the choir and retrochoir of Southwark Cathedral and in St Ethelburga's. Glass became available for the first time since the Romans and churches had tall narrow *lancets*. Soon lancets were grouped together and *window heads* were sometimes pierced with a simple round window (an oculus). Windows grew in complexity and a magnificent *rose window* was a feature of 'Old' St. Paul's Cathedral. Capitals were sometimes decorated in 'stiff-leaf' carvings. Outside simple *pinnacles* were added to buttresses to add weight and slender towers were topped with *spires.*

The word 'decorated' in Decorated Gothic accurately explains the new style which, in France, is even better called 'Flamboyant Gothic'. Windows, in particular, became more elaborate. They were wider than before, usually divided by vertical *mullions* and *cusping* was common. Window heads had elaborate *tracery* often using *trefoil* or quatrefoil shapes and glass was more colourful. The *ogee arch* also appears. Walls had surface decoration such as heraldic shields and capitals were often decorated with naturalistic foliage. Outside, stone decoration was rich and varied and *niches* containing statues of saints were common. Flying buttresses became a flowing decorative feature and towers were elaborately pinnacled. Steep spires and pinnacles had *crockets* on their sloping faces. Many of these features are best seen today in Westminster Abbey. Unfortunately, the other two prestige London buildings of this period, the 'Old' St. Paul's Cathedral and the St. Stephen's Chapel in the Palace of Westminster, have been destroyed by fire.

Late Medieval London

While Decorated Gothic was heavily influenced by the French, Perpendicular Gothic was uniquely English. The chief characteristic of Perpendicular Gothic architecture is that columns, *panelling* and tracery were used to emphasise the height of the ceilings thereby introducing a feeling of light and spaciousness. Another name could however be 'Even-more Decorated' as windows were larger and bar tracery became even more detailed. Window heads were often incorporated into the windows themselves making them massive spider-webs of stone and *fan vaulting* was introduced, sometimes enhanced with elegant *pendants*. Doorways were often surrounded by rectangular frames and *spandrels* became new areas for decoration. Original examples of these features are best seen today in the Henry VII Chapel in Westminster Abbey. However, there are later examples as the Perpendicular Gothic style was to become very popular again in Victorian times with the rebuilt Palace of Westminster a prime example.

Late Medieval domestic houses were usually built of wood although some had stone vaulted cellars. Town houses were often built so that higher storeys overhung lower ones. Over time houses were extended upwards and this led to the roofs of houses on opposite sides of a road almost touching. A characteristic of some important secular buildings in this period are the superb *hammer-beam roofs*, where advances in joinery and a better understanding of how to distribute the load allowed roofs to span greater spaces.

Top spots

Charterhouse, EC1	A chapel was built above a Black Death cemetery and, in 1371, this was expanded into a Carthusian monastery. Some of the monastery walls remain and there is a delightful medieval doorway to a monk's cell in the Norfolk Cloister.
Eltham Palace, SE9	The original palace, which dated from 1290, was a favourite of Henry VIII as a child. Little remains of it today other than the restored Great Hall. A feature of the hall, which was built in the 1470s, is its magnificent oak hammer-beam roof. The hall was badly damaged during the Civil War and was subsequently neglected. The hall and its roof were extensively restored in the 1930s.
Guildhall, EC2	The two crypts with their fine vaulting are thought to date from the 1100s. Much of the Great Hall dates from 1411 although it was restored after the Great Fire (probably by Wren and Hooke) and again after damage in the Second World War.
Jewel Tower, SW1	Built around 1365 to secure Edward III's treasures the tower was known as the 'King's Privy Wardrobe'. The tower is one of only two buildings from the medieval Palace of Westminster to survive the fires of 1512 and 1834. The ground floor features a fine fourteenth-century ribbed vault ceiling with

	bosses. An interesting model of the medieval Palace of Westminster is on show.
Lambeth Palace, SE1	The Archbishop of Canterbury first built a palace at this prime site, directly across the Thames from Westminster, at the end of the twelfth century. The oldest remaining parts are the entrance to Langton's Chapel and the undercroft (now a crypt) beneath it which date to 1220 and are good examples of Early English Gothic architecture. The marble columns with simple rounded capitals are a particular delight. The Guard Room, although restored in 1833, has an original fourteenth-century wooden *arch-braced roof.*
London Wall, EC2	Sections of London's medieval walls remain at Vine Street, Cooper's Row and St Giles Cripplegate but those at Noble Street are probably the most impressive.
Merchant Taylors' Hall, EC2	The hall's crypt was originally part of a late fourteenth-century chapel. It is two *bays* long with ribbed vaulting and carved corbels.
Museum of London, EC2	Museum exhibits include the original statues of Temperance, Fortitude, Justice and Prudence from the 1411 Guildhall Porch and a fine model of the 'Old' St. Paul's Cathedral.
Museum of the Order of St. John, EC1	The Museum tells the story of the Order of St. John spanning almost a thousand years. This fascinating collection is housed in St. John's Gate, a restored gatehouse, which is all that remains of the twelfth-century headquarters of the Knights of St. John.

Palace of Westminster, SW1	St. Stephen's Chapel, built between 1292 and 1348 to emulate Sainte-Chapelle in Paris, was destroyed by the fire of 1834. The crypt of St. Stephen's, now called the Chapel of St. Mary's Undercroft, survived and is one of London's Gothic treasures but, unfortunately, it is difficult for visitors to get access to. Around 1380, Richard II modified Westminster Hall. The Norman roof was replaced with the present oak hammer-beam roof spanning 20 yards and decorated with carvings of angels carrying shields. Windows were added, statues of kings were set in niches and many carvings of a chained deer (Richard's heraldic badge) were displayed on the *cornice*.
Priory Church of St. John, EC1	Beneath the church (a Queen Anne Church that was destroyed in the Blitz), the crypt was constructed in 1220 and was extended in the following century by the addition of two side chapels. As a result, the crypt has both Norman Romanesque and Gothic arches and vaulting. It contains the magnificent tomb of an unknown Spanish knight carved out of a single piece of alabaster.
St. Bartholomew-the-Less, EC1	The church is the latest church associated with St. Bartholomew's Hospital to be built on this site since 1184. The entrance, tower and vestry of the present building are fifteenth-century in origin.

St. Ethelburga's, EC2	This tiny medieval church dates from 1390 but has been extensively restored after being damaged in 1993 by an IRA bomb. The *nave* is separated from the *aisle* by a four-bay *arcade* and there is an early Decorated Gothic five-light window with elaborate bar-tracery, crowned by a large sexfoil (the stained glass in which dates from 1952).
St. Helen's, EC3 **ESSENTIAL**	This delightful church dates from the twelfth century. A priory of Benedictine nuns was built adjoining it in 1210 and, up to the dissolution of the priory in 1538, the church was divided in two by a partition running from east to west with the northern nave serving the nuns and the southern nave the parishioners. The four-bay arcade and the main windows are Decorated Gothic. The church has been called the 'Westminster Abbey of the City' because of its many medieval tombs and monuments (including Thomas Gresham's tomb). The church has been extensively restored after it was badly damaged by IRA bombs.
St. Magnus-the-Martyr, EC3	This Wren church contains a fine model of Peter of Colechurch's first stone London Bridge. Outside the church there are some stones from the old bridge.
Southwark Cathedral, SE1	An important religious building has stood on this site since the seventh century. The Norman Priory of St. Mary Overie ('over the river') and hospital (the predecessor of St. Thomas' Hospital) were severely damaged

	by fire in 1212. While a few Norman doorways remain, much of the east of today's cathedral dates from the Late Medieval period. The choir and the *retrochoir* are Early English Gothic, with their characteristic pointed arches and quadripartite rib vaulting. The altar screen dates from 1520 but many of the statues it holds are newer. The cathedral was extensively restored in Victorian times and much of the west end is Neo-gothic.
Temple Church, EC4 **ESSENTIAL**	The style of the nave differs from that of the *chancel*. The nave is an example of Norman Romanesque, dates from 1185. It was built by the Knights Templar as part of a monastery complex and was designed to recall the circular Church of the Holy Sepulchre in Jerusalem (the holiest place in the Crusaders' world). The chancel was rebuilt about 50 years later. With its rib vaulting and pointed arches it is one of the first examples of Early English Gothic architecture.
Tower of London, EC3	Stone curtain walls with imposing Gothic towers were built in the 1200s creating the first concentric castle in the country (and the prototype for Edward I's castles in North Wales). Entrances, both from the land and the river, were strengthened. The Beauchamp Tower, constructed in the thirteenth century, was the first use of brick

	since Roman times (although it was subsequently faced in stone).
Westminster Abbey, SW1 **ESSENTIAL**	Completed in 1259, the Chapter House was originally used by Benedictine monks for their daily meetings. It is a beautiful octagonal building with an original floor of glazed tiles and 96 wall paintings in the blank arcading. The vaulted ceiling supported by a delicate central column appears later. Much of the rest of Westminster Abbey was built between 1245 and 1270. With its high nave, flying buttresses with pinnacles, rose windows in the transepts and bar tracery it illustrates the transition from Old English to Decorated Gothic. The splendid pavement by the altar, made from marble, glass and stones from Rome, dates from 1268. The west part of the nave was completed in the fourteenth century (except for the towers in the west front which are eighteenth-century).
Winchester Palace, SE1	Only the ruined gable end of the Early English Gothic Great Hall, with a fine rose window, remains of this once large palace complex built as the Archbishop of Winchester's London residence.

Tudor London

Overview of the period between 1485 and 1603

The Tudor dynasty benefitted from an expanding population and strong economic growth. To protect their positions the Tudor monarchs deliberately reduced the power of the nobility and the middle classes grew in number and had more disposable time and income. Trade flourished, agricultural productivity improved and, under Elizabeth, the money supply was augmented by merchant adventurers such as Drake and Raleigh plundering Spanish gold.

In Europe the Renaissance flourished but the renewed interest in classical learning and architecture was limited in England at this time. Indeed, the defining event of the Tudor period was one of separation when the 1534 Act of Supremacy established the Church of England with Henry VIII as its supreme leader on earth. The Dissolution of the Monasteries that closely followed created economic opportunities as many of London's extensive religious properties were transferred to secular use. However, it caused further hardship for the poor as the relief provided by many of the religious groups was terminated. Roman Catholicism returned under Mary and many were executed for their Protestant beliefs. Although her successor, Elizabeth, was Protestant she inherited a bitterly divided kingdom. To avoid a return to Catholicism she needed an active web of informers and good fortune in defeating the Spanish Armada.

Both Henry VII and Henry VIII were profligate with regard to their own accommodation. Architecture was used by the Tudors to project power both within Britain and, especially when Cardinal Wolsey was Lord Chancellor, internationally. Palaces were built, or sequestrated, in

47

London (Whitehall and St. James'), Greenwich, Richmond, Ewell and at Hampton Court. Urbanisation increased and London's population grew substantially although people largely still lived within the City boundaries.

Growth, trading and finance

Despite plague attacks in 1563 and 1603 London's population grew from about 50,000 to 200,000 during the Tudor period. It was fuelled by immigration both from within England (stimulated by widespread land enclosure[27]) and overseas (especially from the Netherlands). Southwark was formally incorporated into London in 1550 but Westminster remained separate.

Government and the legal system became more centralised, organised and bureaucratic and courtiers, litigants and their retinues were drawn to London. Rich and poor lived side by side in the medieval city with its wooden buildings, narrow unsanitary streets and an absence of public spaces. The Lord Mayor and the City authorities discouraged expansion outside the City boundaries and therefore beyond their power. This policy was supported by Elizabeth. In 1580 she ordered that no new houses should be built within three miles of the City unless on the site of an existing building. Peter of Colechurch's medieval London Bridge remained the only river bridge but it was congested and costly and most people preferred to be ferried across the Thames in wherries. There was an improvement in the supply of 'fresh' water to the city when, in the 1580s, Thames water started to be pumped to Cornhill powered by water wheels located under London Bridge.

London prospered under the Tudors and, other than when Mary ruled, the monarchy was popular with Londoners. Henry VIII secured a free trade treaty with the Netherlands, the navy was strengthened and, especially under Elizabeth, merchant adventurers such as Drake and Raleigh were encouraged to plunder Spanish gold and silver, much of which ended up in the capital. In the 1540s almost 90% of England's exports of woollen cloth passed through the city with much of it destined for Antwerp. Linen, iron, hemp and manufactured goods were imported.

Trading companies such as the Muscovy Company (1553), the Levant Company (1581) and the East India Company (1600) were established initially through merchants being granted monopolies by the Crown. In time, the wealthy could invest in these companies and spread their risk by the new device of purchasing a share of the joint stock. These shares were traded and early financial markets evolved. The Royal Exchange, an area where merchants, ship owners and financiers could meet and do business, was opened by Thomas Gresham in 1571.

The growth of London as a port provided a valuable opportunity to raise tax. In 1559 an Act of Parliament established new rules for customs tax. One of the more important provisions was that it became illegal to land or load goods anywhere other than at specified 'Legal Quays' under the supervision of customs officers. In London, Legal Quays were established on the north bank of the Thames between London Bridge and the Tower of London. This short stretch of wharves was to be London's only port until the early nineteenth century. In 1513 naval dockyards were established at Woolwich and Deptford. Many warships were constructed there and in 1578 a dry dock was constructed to facilitate ship repairs. Later Chatham also became a major naval dockyard.

Impact of the Reformation

In 1534, largely due to Henry VIII's difficulties in obtaining a divorce from Catherine of Aragon, the Roman Catholic church was replaced by the Protestant Church of England with the monarch as its Supreme Head. While this coincided with the Luther inspired Reformation movement[28] the circumstances and consequences in England differed from those elsewhere in Northern Europe. In England change to the style of religious worship was slow and the most immediate action was the Crown's appropriation of much of the church's wealth.

Master-minded by Thomas Cromwell, the Dissolution of the Monasteries resulted in huge amounts of church land and property, especially from the monasteries, being sold between 1536 and 1540. Much of this land was built upon and this robbed the city of many of its open spaces. The loss of the monasteries also caused a breakdown in London's systems for education and social welfare. While Edward VI founded some schools such as Christ's Hospital School in the old Grey Friars' buildings at Newgate, it fell to the merchants and their guilds to fill the vacuum. Many of the schools that were formed during the Reformation remain today, albeit relocated, including Christ's Hospital, Charterhouse, St. Paul's, the City of London and Merchant Taylors' Schools. Little was done to replace the relief that the monasteries provided to the poor.

Numerous Tudor palaces

Palaces were an important symbol of power for the Tudors. Henry VII built Richmond Palace[29] and renovated Greenwich Palace.[30] In 1512, during the early years of the reign of Henry VIII, fire destroyed the royal residential area of Westminster Palace. As a replacement St. James' Palace was built and, in 1534, Henry VIII appropriated York Place from

Cardinal Wolsey. Renamed the Palace of Whitehall, Henry used this as his principal residence and it grew to become the largest palace in Europe with over 1,500 rooms and covering 23 acres. Westminster remained in use for Parliament and the Royal Courts of Law. Enriched by the funds obtained from the Dissolution of the Monasteries, Henry VIII built on an unprecedented scale. By his death in 1547 he owned over 20 houses in the London area and Nonsuch Palace[31] in Ewell. Apart from Hampton Court and St. James' Palace little remains of these properties today.

Gatehouse to St. Bartholomew-the-Great

New forms of entertainment

Elizabeth I's accession to the throne saw the heyday of English theatre. Londoners flocked to Southwark where there were a number of theatres including the Hope, the Swan, and the two where Shakespeare worked most, the Rose and the Globe. Other forms of entertainment were also readily available in Southwark such as pleasure gardens, taverns and alehouses, bear baiting and cock-fighting. Then, of course, there were the brothels. Southwark was famous for its ladies of the night who worked from the 'stews' located in properties owned by the Bishop of Winchester. The tensions between this hedonism and the growing Puritan movement were increasingly to be seen under the Stuart monarchs.

Timeline

	National events	London events
1485	Henry VII crowned	
1500		Greenwich Palace built
1503		Building of the Henry VII Chapel at Westminster Abbey commenced
1509	Henry VIII crowned	
1512		Fire destroys much of Westminster Palace
1534	Act of Supremacy passed	Henry VIII occupies the Palace of Whitehall
1535	Execution of Thomas More	
1536	Dissolution of the Monasteries commences	
1547	Edward VI crowned	
1553	Mary crowned	
1558	Elizabeth I crowned	
1563		Plague kills about 25% of London's population
1571		The Royal Exchange opened
1588	Spanish Armada defeated	
1603	Death of Elizabeth I brings the Tudor period to a close	Plague kills about 20% of London's population

Tudor London

Tudor architecture

In the sixteenth century the glories of the Renaissance, which first flowered in fifteenth-century Italy, spread throughout Continental Europe. However, Henry VIII's break with Rome meant that England entered a period of cultural isolation which deferred the impact of this renewed interest in classical architecture. Although peripheral classical ornamentation was sometimes added to new buildings such as Nonsuch Palace, the primary architectural style remained Gothic. Changes in style included the pointed arch giving way to the flattened Tudor arch and the advent of *oriel windows*. Good examples of oriel windows can be seen above Traitors' Gate in the Tower of London and in the church of St. Bartholomew-the-Great.

The Tudor period saw much building of royal palaces and grand houses for the aristocracy and the nouveau riche. The spectacular Henry VII Chapel was added to Westminster Abbey but, after the Act of Supremacy, there was relatively little church building within London. The main architectural innovation of the period was the use of bricks. Introduced from the Low Countries, brick became one of the most common building materials in Tudor London. Good examples of brick buildings are St. James' Palace and the gateway to Lambeth Palace. Both retain some of the original diapering (diamond shapes in burnt brick) that was a popular decoration.

Many Tudor houses were wood framed with white-washed lath and plaster infill between the beams thereby creating the famous 'black and white' appearance. A few examples remain today within the Tower of London, in Fleet Street and the gatehouse of St. Bartholomew-the-Great.

Traitors' Gate from inside the Tower of London

The widespread adoption of coal as fuel meant that chimneys and enclosed fireplaces became common for the first time. Chimney stacks were often clustered in groups, and chimney columns were variously curved, twisted, and decorated with chequerboard patterns made from bricks of different colours.

Top spots

Charterhouse, EC1	Lord Edward North, who administered much of the Dissolution of the Monasteries, rewarded himself with this property in 1545 and built a large courtyard house. The Great Hall, with its arch-braced roof, and the Great Chamber, with its fine ceiling, remain. The washhouse complex has some delightful Tudor brickwork and the Norfolk Cloister has brick vaulting dating from this period.
Chelsea Old Church, SW3	Chelsea Old Church dates from 1157 and was the parish church of Chelsea village before it was engulfed by London. The building originally consisted of a thirteenth-century chancel and a nave with chapels to the north and south. The chapel to the south was rebuilt in 1528 as Sir Thomas More's private chapel. The church was badly damaged in the Second World War but the More Chapel largely survived.
Globe Theatre, SE1	First built in 1599 the theatre had covered galleries but an open stage. It burnt down in 1613 but was soon rebuilt. Today's Globe Theatre is a twentieth-century reconstruction.
Lambeth Palace, SE1	The imposing Morton's Tower, built in 1496, and the Cranmer Tower are red brick. Both show some of the original diapering that was a popular Tudor decoration.
Middle Temple Hall, EC4	The Elizabethan Middle Temple Hall was built between 1562 and 1573 and remains virtually unchanged having survived the Great Fire. The

	hall is notable for its fine double hammer-beam roof, carved screen and wood panelling.
Old Cock Tavern, Fleet Street, EC4	Two of the remaining black and white façades are close to each other on Fleet Street. The Old Cock Tavern at number 22 has a fine exterior dated 1549. Almost next door, the house at number 17 was built in 1610. Inside, the Prince Henry room (not open to the public) has a highly decorated Jacobean plaster ceiling.
St. Andrew Undershaft, EC3	Built in the 1520s, the church survived both the Great Fire and the 1940 Blitz but was badly damaged by an IRA bomb. The tower and interior are Perpendicular Gothic and the flat ceiling, although restored, is typical of the Tudor period. The heraldic glass in the aisle windows dates from 1530.
St. Bartholomew-the-Great, EC1	The oriel window on the south side of the choir dates from 1517 and the black and white gatehouse from 1595.
St. James' Palace, SW1	Mainly built between 1531 and 1536, the brick palace was secondary in importance to the Palace of Whitehall for most Tudor and Stuart monarchs. It has two chapels of note. The Chapel Royal (not to be confused with the one in the Tower of London) was built in 1540. The Queen's Chapel, completed in 1625, was designed by Inigo Jones for the Roman Catholic Queen Henrietta Maria. St. James' Palace grew in importance during the reigns of the early Georgian monarchs, but was eventually displaced by Buckingham Palace.

St. John's Gate, EC1	The brick and ragstone gate was the main entrance to the Priory of St. John. It was destroyed in the Peasants' Revolt and then rebuilt in 1504. While the substance of the current gate is Tudor it was extensively restored in 1903.
St. Margaret's Westminster, SW1	Completed in 1523, the parish church of Parliament has been extensively modified over the years. The most notable Tudor feature is the stained glass in the east window which commemorates the marriage of Henry VIII (or perhaps his brother Arthur) to Catherine of Aragon.
St. Martin-in-the-Fields, WC2	Henry VIII built a church here in 1542 to prevent bodies of plague victims from having to pass through the Palace of Whitehall. At this time it was an isolated position between the cities of Westminster and London - literally 'in the fields'. The Tudor church was demolished in 1720 and only the fine red brick rib vaulted crypt remains today.
Staple Inn Chambers, WC1	Dating from 1585, the building was once the wool staple, the location where wool was weighed and taxed. It survived the Great Fire but was modified by the Victorians and extensively damaged by bombing. After the Second World War the façade was restored in the Tudor black and white style.
Sutton House, E9	While this Elizabethan merchant's house is not the grandest of National Trust properties, its oak panelled 'linen fold' room is magnificent and there is some interesting information on, and

	examples of, Tudor bricks. The thirteenth-century tower of St. Augustine's Church is nearby.
Tower of London, EC3 **ESSENTIAL**	Roofs were added to the four turrets of the White Tower in the 1530s and windows were added around 1638. The impressive Queen's House was built in about 1540 facing Tower Green. There are also some fine black and white Tudor buildings backing onto Bayward Tower and brickwork above Traitors' Gate. Also dating from this period is the church of St. Peter ad Vincula. This Chapel Royal is built in the Perpendicular Gothic style and is the burial site of Henry VIII's decapitated wives. It contains some fine monuments, a Tudor font and a Grinling Gibbons organ.
Westminster Abbey, SW1 **ESSENTIAL**	The Henry VII Chapel was built between 1503 and 1519 and is an excellent example of late Perpendicular Gothic architecture. The fan vaulted ceiling with pendants is spectacular as are the traceried windows although unfortunately little remains of the original Tudor stained glass. The exterior with its abundant decoration is just as exuberant with the chapel's height being emphasised by weight bearing piers fashioned as octagonal turrets capped by ogee shaped domes.

Stuart London

Overview of the period between 1603 and 1714

The death of the heirless Elizabeth in 1603 created a constitutional crisis that was resolved by inviting James VI of Scotland to become James I of England. James, great-great-grandson of Henry VII, was the son of Mary Queen of Scots and Henry Stuart. The Stuart family was to rule for most of the seventeenth century. This was a turbulent period in British history. There was continuing friction between the Catholic and Protestant religions and between England and Scotland and Ireland. There was a civil war, a short period as a republic, the restoration of the monarchy and then a 'Glorious Revolution'. In successive years London suffered the twin devastations of the Great Plague and the Great Fire.

Despite all this London's population grew from 200,000 to 500,000 and London expanded beyond its old boundaries. For the first time, rich and poor started to live in different areas of the city with the wealthy occupying new areas such as Covent Garden, Haymarket and Bloomsbury. The Great Fire forced an upgrade in the quality of buildings and gave Christopher Wren the opportunity to create a new London skyline by rebuilding St. Paul's Cathedral and many churches in the fashionable Baroque style.

Growing political unrest

Superficially life in London under the early Stuarts was probably not so dissimilar from that experienced under the Tudors. Whitehall Palace continued to be the centre of power and was graced by the addition of the magnificent Banqueting House for welcoming ambassadors and for holding masques. The East India Company flourished and, after the

Virginia Company was founded in 1606, trade with America and the Caribbean rapidly grew. There were good profits to be made from tobacco and sugar. Immigration continued including Dutch protestants who brought with them knowledge about horticulture and the use of human manure to improve productivity. Around this time, the delightfully named Dung Wharf was used to move excrement from the city to the market gardens in what is today Battersea, Fulham and Chelsea.

Wealthy Londoners started to live further to the west where there was more space and better supplies of clean water.[32] This was facilitated by the invention of coaches with first leather, and then metal, springs with revolutionised transport for the privileged. The first major property development was in Covent Garden in 1632 when, encouraged by Charles I, the Duke of Bedford was granted a licence to build a residential piazza. Rows of brick houses formed streets with the names of Henrietta, Charles, James, King and York indicating the importance of maintaining royal patronage. Long Acre and St. Martin's Lane developments soon followed and, after the Civil War, there was further building in Soho, St. Giles and Westminster.

However, Londoners were to become disenchanted with James I and more especially his son, Charles I. There was opposition to James's wish to form a union between England and Scotland and the elite were angry that the impecunious Stuart monarchs looked for every possible way of raising money at their expense. To make matters worse the Stuarts were bad for business as the navy was allowed to decline with the consequence that piracy was hitting trading profits. The poor were becoming increasingly intoxicated by Puritan[33] thinking and were antagonistic towards the Crown's excesses and tolerance of Catholicism. Tensions between the monarchy and Parliament also grew. James I and Charles I were firm believers in the 'Divine Right of Kings' and resented what they saw as Parliament's interference. There were many angry disagreements and Parliament was suspended for long periods.[34] In 1642 Charles I took soldiers to the Palace of Westminster in an attempt to arrest five members of parliament. He failed, the mob was incited and Charles fled the capital. The Civil War had started.

London in the Civil War

During the Civil War the Puritan Common Council took control of London and the city became a crucial source of funding for Parliament. After initial Royalist victories, a hastily organised London militia of 24,000 men blocked Charles' forces at Turnham Green. [35] This was to be Charles' last chance of taking London and, without the City's wealth, the Royalists could not win the war. Londoners were however not to know this and the authorities hastened to construct earth ramparts, enhanced with bastions and redoubts. Protected by these defensive earthworks[36] it is ironic that the only real damage to the capital was to the interiors of Westminster Abbey and Lambeth Palace which were ill-treated by Parliamentary forces who were billetted there. Taken prisoner in 1647, Charles was tried for high treason in Westminster Hall and executed outside the Banqueting House in January 1649.

Thereafter Oliver Cromwell[37] ruled the country virtually as a dictator and several royal palaces, including Richmond, were demolished. While the Navigation Acts[38] and an aggressive foreign policy against the Dutch pleased London's merchants, the elite were worried about an erosion of their power. This was also a fairly dismal time for ordinary Londoners. Strong Puritan moral values were enforced, theatres were closed, Christmas was not celebrated and the consumption of alcohol was prohibited (this at least encouraged coffee to be drunk and the first coffee houses were opened). In the political void created by Cromwell's death in 1658, Parliament commenced negotiations with Charles II to return from exile in Holland.

Renovation in the Restoration

The reign of Charles II saw a dramatic swing in moral values. Charles himself illustrated the permissive standards of the time by having multiple mistresses and making no secret of his fourteen illegitimate children (one of whom was the infamous Duke of Monmouth). London theatres reopened and bawdy 'Restoration comedy' was very popular especially at the new Theatre Royal in Drury Lane. The Mall was constructed for promenades and St. James' Park was laid out with formal avenues and a long canal. Despite all the fun the period is probably best remembered for two disasters: The Great Plague and, in the following year, the Great Fire. In 1665 Bubonic plague killed about 100,000 Londoners (perhaps 20% of the population) with bodies being dumped in mass burial sites. The following year fire[39] destroyed most of the medieval city. While many private houses were rebuilt within five years, public buildings such as the churches and St. Paul's Cathedral, that needed to be funded by a tax on coal, were to take up to 40 years.

Rebuilding the city after the Great Fire was a major challenge. Many ideas were offered for a complete redesign of London but, due to a lack of funding and the impediment of pre-existing property rights, the city was largely rebuilt along the established road system. Some improvements were however made. Most streets (such as Cheapside) were widened, pavements were added and King Street and Queen Street were newly created (this must have been at the behest of the Livery Companies as the streets make a fantastic approach from the Thames to Guildhall!). Importantly, Thames Street was widened improving access to the port facilities. Although it escaped serious damage in 1666, Temple Bar was rebuilt.

Temple Bar, Paternoster Square

Immediately following the fire reconstruction within the City boundaries was closely controlled[40] and much of the area could not be occupied. There was rapid property development[41] in areas such as Holborn, Clerkenwell and Bloomsbury, expansion to the north in Hackney, Shoreditch and Spitalfields as well as new settlements to the east in Ratcliffe, Wapping and Shadwell and around the new shipbuilding activity at Blackwall. By 1700 perhaps 40% of London's population was living outside the City boundaries and, much to the Lord Mayor's chagrin, beyond the power of the City authorities.

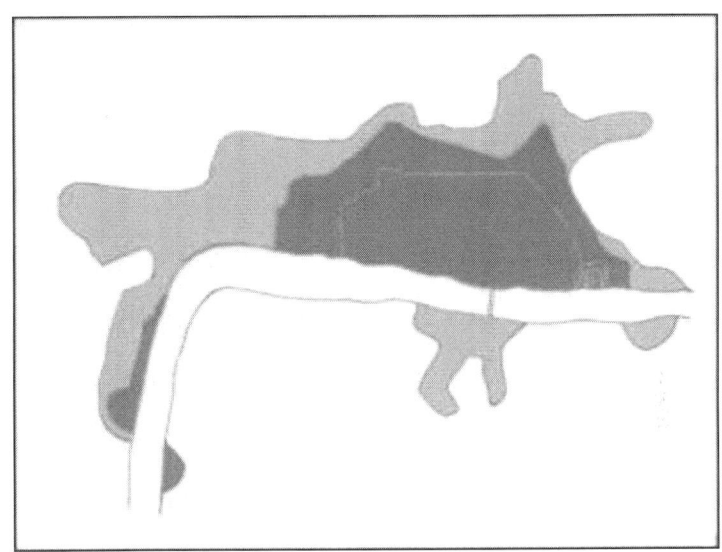

**Populated area in 1700 showing the expansion (light grey)
since 1485**

By the middle of the seventeenth century London's trading network had expanded. The success of the East India and Virginia Companies meant that a third of the city's trade was now with Asia and America with significant imports of tobacco, sugar, textiles and the newly fashionable coffee and tea. Many of these goods were re-exported to Continental Europe. Immigration was high and many French Huguenots arrived following Louis XIV's revocation of the Edict of Nantes in 1685. The Huguenots[42] were energetic and skilled and established a silk industry at Spitalfields and Shoreditch.

However, a prosperous London did not mean a wealthy monarchy. Indeed, Charles II was so much in debt that in 1672 he needed to suspend repayment of his debts for a year and five leading goldsmith bankers went bankrupt. There was a growing need for a national bank whose financial affairs could be distanced from the vagaries of royal finances. However, political uncertainties meant that the creation of the Bank of England[43] in 1694 needed to await the stability provided by William III and, perhaps, the knowledge of the more advanced Dutch banking practices that came with him.

London after the Glorious Revolution

There was continuing tension between the Catholic and Protestant religions. Both Charles II and his brother James II were closet Catholics. In 1688, to defend the Anglican Church, Parliament invited the Dutch William of Orange to invade and James fled without offering resistance. William ruled as William III of England alongside his wife Mary, James II's Protestant daughter. In 1701, Protestant rule was mandated by the Act of Settlement.

William III was not fond of London life and its smog exacerbated his asthma. After a catastrophic fire at Whitehall Palace in 1698 William and Mary moved their court to Kensington, then a village on the edge of London. This was another step in the expansion of London and more work for Christopher Wren. Wren was also involved with the construction of the Greenwich Royal Hospital for Seamen and the Royal Hospital, Chelsea.

By the late seventeenth century London was a thriving location for commerce. The Royal Exchange continued as a location where merchants, brokers and ship-owners could trade and exchange information about ship arrivals and commodity prices. Trade credit and marine insurance was becoming increasingly important and banking started to evolve. There was active trading in shares in the East India Company and the South Sea Company.[44] Much of this financial business was conducted in coffee houses.[45] The first recorded trading in shares took place in 1698 in Jonathan's coffee house, Change Alley and insurance deals started in Lloyd's coffee house in Tower Street.

Timeline

	National events	London events
1603	James I, the first Stuart king, crowned	
1606	Virginia Company founded	
1622		Banqueting House completed
1625	Charles I crowned	
1632		Covent Garden piazza built
1642	Civil War commenced	Stand-off at Turnham Green
1649	Charles I executed	
1653	Oliver Cromwell made Lord Protector	First coffee house opened
1660	The Restoration and Charles II crowned	
1665		The Great Plague
1666		The Great Fire
1681		Royal Hospital, Chelsea founded

1685	Monmouth Rebellion	
1688	The Glorious Revolution and William III crowned	
1689		William acquires Kensington Palace
1694		Establishment of the Bank of England and building of Greenwich Royal Hospital for Seamen commenced
1698		Whitehall Palace destroyed by fire
1701	Act of Settlement	
1702	Queen Anne crowned	
1707	Act of Union with Scotland	
1711		Completion of St. Paul's Cathedral
1714	Death of Queen Anne brings an end to the Stuart dynasty	

Stuart Architecture

A number of early Stuart buildings, such as Lincoln's Inn Chapel, continued to be built in the Gothic style. However, fashions were to change and the Classical styles of the European Renaissance movement finally came to be appreciated. There were two main styles – the Palladian and the Baroque. The Palladian style, with Inigo Jones[46] as its main proponent, was based on the formal *Classical Orders* used in Greek and Roman temple architecture. It used rounded arches, *colonnades*, *pilasters*, *pediments, porticos* and often *rustication* and emphasis was placed on symmetry and mathematical proportions. London has the Banqueting House, the Queen's House in Greenwich and the Queen's Chapel in St. James' Palace as fine examples. After the Civil War the Baroque style became dominant, especially for church architecture. This was less formal in the way in which classical devices were combined and gave more emphasis to light and colour. The Palladian style was to return to popularity in the eighteenth century.

The Great Fire provided an opportunity for Wren and others. In total 49 of the 87 London churches that had been destroyed were rebuilt, mostly in the English Baroque style. English Baroque church architecture tended to be relatively simple in comparison with other European countries and was intended to promote the Protestant ethic of the priest seeking to engage a congregation rather than awe inspire it. Interiors were simple and bright, with decoration mostly in the ceiling designs. Most churches had galleries and wooden pulpits, *testers* and *reredoses* (the best carved by Grinling Gibbons) and there were no rood screens. Windows were generally plain glass. Outside *steeples* were used rather than *domes*, probably because medieval stone church towers generally survived the Great Fire and were incorporated into the new designs. However, a massive dome featured very prominently in Wren's grandest construction, St. Paul's Cathedral. Domes in St.

69

Stephen's Walbrook and St. Mary Abchurch illustrate the evolution of Wren's thinking for his great work. While some of Wren's work remains, much was modified by the Victorians or destroyed by bombing in the Second World War. The three most 'authentic' Wren interiors are thought to be St. James' Church Garlickhythe, St. Mary Abchurch and St. Mary-at-Hill. In the early eighteenth century Baroque styles became more elaborate, especially in Hawksmoor's Queen Anne Churches

Wren steeples: St. Bride's, St. Mary-le-Bow and St. Magnus-the-Martyr

The Low Countries were also an influence on architecture at this time. The *Dutch gable,* as featured in Holland House, had arrived in Britain during the latter part of the sixteenth century and Dutch architecture became increasingly popular under William III and Queen Anne. What is today known as the Queen Anne style evolved with brickwork using the 'Flemish bond', sash windows being set flush with the brickwork, stone quoins emphasising corners, hipped roofs and dormer windows. Queen Anne's Gate, SW1, is a good example of a terrace of this period.

Top spots

Banqueting House, SW1 ****ESSENTIAL****	Completed in 1622, the Banqueting House is the only remaining part of the Palace of Whitehall. Designed by Inigo Jones in the Palladian style, the exterior has both *Ionic* and *Corinthian* capitals, alternating rounded and pointed window pediments and an attractive frieze of fruits. The building was re-faced in Portland stone in the Victorian period but the details of the original façade were preserved. Charles I commissioned Rubens to paint nine magnificent canvases for the ceiling. Installed in 1636, these splendid works glorify both James I and the union of the crowns of England and Scotland.
Charterhouse, EC1	In 1611 the site was acquired by the wealthy Thomas Sutton and, after his death, become an almshouse and school. The monk's chapter house was converted into a chapel which is dominated by a fine monument to Sutton.
Covent Garden, WC2	A three-sided residential piazza, designed by Inigo Jones, was built in 1632 with St. Paul's Church on the fourth side. By 1670 the space in the middle started to be used as a fruit, vegetable and flower market. All that remains today of the original development is St. Paul's Church (see below) but the modern arcaded buildings on the north side echo the original piazza.
George Inn, SE1	This is one of the few ancient coaching inns to survive in Greater London and is the only galleried example. The inn dates from 1542 but

	was rebuilt after the Great Fire of Southwark in 1676.
Holland House, W14	Built in 1606, the house was largely destroyed in the Blitz. Today only the east wing of the building remains, with its fine Dutch gables. A pair of *Doric* column stone gate pillars designed by Inigo Jones also survive.
Kensington Palace, W8 **ESSENTIAL**	In 1689 William and Mary used Wren and Hawksmoor to remodel Nottingham House (originally built in 1605) to be their new palace in Kensington. In order to save time and money, the Jacobean house was left to form the core and four, three storey, pavilions were added at the corners. The wood panelled Queen's State Apartments date from this time as does much of the rather uninspiring exterior. Fine gardens were laid out and a separate Orangery was added by Queen Anne in 1705.
Lambeth Palace, SE1	The Great Hall was ransacked by Cromwellian troops during the Civil War and was rebuilt in 1663. It has a fine Gothic hammer-beam roof and, inset into it, is a very 'Wren-like' *lantern light*.
Lincoln's Inn Chapel, WC2	The chapel was built between 1620 and 1623 but has been extensively modified subsequently. The side windows contain some seventeenth-century stained glass and there are some original high pews with doors. However, the highlight is the fan vaulted, open undercroft.
Museum of London, EC2	Museum exhibits include a fine model of the Great Fire and Oliver Cromwell's death mask.

Queen Anne's Gate, SW1	These superb terrace houses were built in 1705. Many are five storey buildings using both red and dark brown bricks. A number have elaborate wooden door canopies and lower floor windows have key stones with faces carved on them.
Queen's House Greenwich, SE10 **ESSENTIAL**	Completed in 1635 for the wife of James I, this was one of the first Palladian style buildings designed by Inigo Jones. The interior, which Charles II had remodelled in 1662, is especially fine with carved ceilings, black and white marble floor tiles and a grand spiral staircase (called the 'Tulip Staircase' but actually the flower is a lily!). Outside there are colonnades to either side and a high balustrade hides the roof.
Royal Hospital, Chelsea, SW3	Designed by Wren, the Royal Hospital opened its doors in 1692 to provide relief for about 500 army veterans, some injured at the recent Battle of Sedgemoor. The red brick hospital has a central section containing the Great Hall and chapel and four projecting accommodation wings. Each veteran was given a small berth formed from wooden partitions placed back to back against a central wall. The beautiful chapel has double height windows and an impressive mural of The Resurrection.
Royal Hospital for Seamen, Greenwich, SE10	The Tudor palace of Greenwich was demolished and what is now the King Charles Block was built in 1664. This was incorporated into the Royal Hospital for Seamen, construction of which was phased between 1694 and 1742. To maintain the river view from the Queen's House, the

(also known as the Old Royal Naval College) **ESSENTIAL**	hospital was built in four blocks. The riverside buildings are the original King Charles Block and the Queen Anne Block and behind them are the domed Queen Mary and King William Blocks. The King Charles Block was designed by Webb (a pupil of Inigo Jones), the others were designed by a combination of Wren, Hawksmoor and Vanbrugh. Between 1873 and 1998 the buildings were used as the Royal Navy College.
St. Bride's, EC4	As can be seen in the crypt, several churches have existed on this site since early Saxon times. The present church, designed by Wren in the Baroque style, was completed in 1678. It is famous for its tall spire with five octagonal stages of diminishing sizes (the 'wedding-cake') which was added in 1701. The building was burnt down in the Second World War and was extensively restored in 1957. Wren's proportions and brightness have been retained but the furnishing is modern.
St. Clement Danes, WC2	It is thought that St. Clement's was originally built by Vikings in the ninth century and a church is mentioned in the Domesday Book. For nearly 150 years it was in the care of the Knights Templar. The church escaped damage in the Great Fire but was rebuilt in 1681 to a Wren design. In 1941 incendiary bombs gutted the building leaving only the walls and tower standing. In the 1950s the church was sympathetically restored.
St. Katharine Cree, EC3	Originally a priory church, St Katharine Cree was rebuilt in 1628 by Archbishop Laud in a

	transitional style that differs from the wave of Baroque churches that was soon to follow. The interior has Gothic ribbed vaulting with bosses and the extensive tracery of the east window was modelled on the much larger rose window in 'Old' St. Paul's Cathedral. The ceiling is however flattened and the arcades are Classical with round *coffered* arches supported by Corinthian columns.
St. Magnus – the – Martyr, EC3 **ESSENTIAL**	This was one of the first buildings to be destroyed in the Great Fire as it stood less than 300 yards from the source in Pudding Lane. Wren's work on rebuilding the church was substantially complete by 1676 but the famous steeple was not finished until 1706. While, over time, there have been extensive modifications, the interior remains a blaze of white and gold. The central bay on the north side survives with its pedimented doorway and swag decoration and the pulpit, tester and the lower part of the dominant two-storey reredos are also original.
St. Margaret's Lothbury, EC2	Built by Wren between 1686 and 1690, the church has exceptionally fine woodwork moved from other, now-demolished, churches. These include the reredos and spiral communion rails which are thought to be carved by Grinling Gibbons (from St Olave, Old Jewry) and the pulpit, tester and rood screen (from All-Hallows-the-Great).
St. Martin-within-Ludgate, EC4	Designed by Wren and Hooke, the church was completed in 1703 and survived the Second World War intact. It is topped by a lead-covered

	octagonal cupola supporting a balcony and tapered spire rising to a height of 158 feet. The interior is in the form of a Greek cross with barrel vaulted arms meeting in a groin vaulted crossing supported by four large Corinthian columns.
St. Mary Abchurch, EC4 **ESSENTIAL**	This small and delightfully simple church has no columns and no aisles but is does have a dome - one of the few examples in a Wren church. The painted dome is carried by eight modest arches. The steeple has an ogee-domed base, a small pierced lantern and an obelisk spire. The church largely survived the Second World War and the original woodwork is spectacular including high pews, a fine pulpit and a Gibbons' reredos.
St. Mary Aldermary, EC4	A rare example of a Wren church in the Perpendicular Gothic style. The tower's corner buttresses rise to four pinnacles. The interior has six Gothic arches and wide aisles. The highlight is the magnificent plaster ceiling with impressive saucer-like mouldings and fan vaulting.
St. Paul's Cathedral, EC4 **ESSENTIAL**	After the Great Fire, there was much debate about the style in which St. Paul's should be rebuilt. A number of Wren's early designs were rejected. Rebuilding started in 1675 and was completed in 1711. Its grandeur is helped by the outer walls being carried to their full height hiding the underlying flying buttresses. The magnificent west façade, the most familiar face of the cathedral, has two tiers of Classical columns under the pediment which is flanked by

	substantial Baroque towers. The vast, triple-layered dome that crowns the cathedral is second in size only to St. Peter's in the Vatican.
St. Paul's, Covent Garden, WC2	Built in 1632, St. Paul's Church was the fourth side of a residential piazza designed by Inigo Jones. The portico is formed of four Tuscan columns supporting a large plain pediment. To the modern eye, the façade may seem rather heavy but it is lightened by flanking gates and corner houses that also emphasise the Palladian symmetry. Known as the 'Actors' Church', the interior is rather austere.
St. Stephen's, Walbrook, EC4 **ESSENTIAL**	The church was completed in 1679 to a Wren Baroque design and the steeple was added in 1717. The church is renowned for its fine proportions and the way its square interior is combined with its round dome. The dome (a prototype for St. Paul's Cathedral) is supported by eight semi-circular arches sitting on four groups of three slender Corinthian columns. Four more columns complete the nave. Other features of note are the coffered plasterwork of the dome and the original woodwork including a substantial door case, a fine reredos and pulpit and a tester with its ogee dome.
Temple Bar Arch, EC4	Commissioned by Charles II and attributed to Wren, this fine Baroque arch of Portland stone was constructed between 1669 and 1672. It spanned Fleet Street until it was replaced in 1878 in order to improve the traffic flow. However, the gateway was preserved and in 1994 it was re-erected in Paternoster Square.

The Monument, EC3	Designed by Wren and Hooke and built between 1671 and 1677, The Monument is a Doric column topped with a flaming urn in gilt bronze. The frieze shows Liberty, Architecture and Science advising Charles II and his brother, James, on the rebuilding of the city. The Monument is 202 feet tall and is located 202 feet to the west of the bakehouse in Pudding Lane where the fire started. There is a fine view from the top but 311 steps to climb first!
Ye Olde Cheshire Cheese, EC4	Rebuilt soon after the Great Fire, the interior of the pub has remainded largely unchanged ever since. The vaulted cellars are thought to date to the thirteenth century when a Carmelite monastery occupied the site.
York House Watergate, WC2	Built in 1626 this was a river entrance to the Duke of Buckingham's palace and is one of the few surviving reminders of the Italianate court style of Charles I. Its rusticated design and scallop shell carvings have been variously attributed to Inigo Jones, Sir Balthazar Gerbier and to Nicholas Stone. Its location in Embankment Gardens is a vivid illustration of just how far the north bank of the Thames has moved south over the years.

Georgian London

Overview of the period between 1714 and 1810

Queen Anne died without an heir in 1714 and George, the Elector of Hanover and great grandson of James I, became an unpopular king known for his unsociable behaviour and difficulty with the English language. Not surprisingly George disliked England and spent much of his time in Hanover. His son, another George, also disliked him - poor relations between the monarch and the Prince of Wales became a recurring theme of the Georgian period! George II was only marginally more popular than his father especially after his wife, Queen Caroline, died in 1737 and he surrounded himself with German courtiers and spent as much time as possible in Hanover. These absences cleared the way for Prime Ministers such as Robert Walpole and the Earl of Chatham (William Pitt the Elder) to take control. George III tried to wrestle back power and this led to a period of political instability.

Britain's Empire was largely formed in the eighteenth century. Britain was at war with France for much of it, with most of the fighting taking place at sea and in the new colonies. The Treaty of Utrecht in 1713 advanced British expansion in North America and in 1763 the Treaty of Paris gave Britain effective control of that continent and also consolidated British influence in India. While war and Britain's strong navy was a major factor in gaining new territory, exploration also played a role especially in 1769 when James Cook reached Australia and claimed it for Britain. The American War of Independence (1776 – 1783) led to the loss of the American colonies. George III's bouts of apparent insanity commenced soon afterwards and England was fortunate to have William Pitt the Younger who became Prime Minister in 1783 at the age of 24. He was able to steer the country through a turbulent period which included the French Revolution and the start of the long war with Napoleon.

Facilitated by improved roads and new bridges, London rapidly expanded in all directions and property developers flourished. Capitalism was rampant and trade expanded especially with the new colonies. The West Indian plantations, and the slave trade that supported them, were a major source of wealth. For the affluent and the expanding middle class the quality of life improved. However, there was still chronic poverty in Georgian London and, as wealth moved west, the poorer parishes in the east entered a downward spiral of poverty, disease and lawlessness.

London expands in all directions

London's population grew from about 500,000 to 1,000,000. Much of this was the result of immigration, especially from Scotland and Ireland. The very poor St. Giles parish (just to the north of Covent Garden) housed many of the unskilled Irish Catholics and others lived in and around Wapping, where the ports were an important source of employment. The Huguenot and Jewish communities also grew but immigrants were not always welcome. In 1780 London was rocked by the Gordon Riots,[47] an uprising of the mob objecting to Roman Catholic emancipation.

St. James' Palace and the Prince of Wales' neighbouring residence, Carlton House,[48] acted as a magnet for new housing development. Soon building commenced in Mayfair and Piccadilly as wealthy families leased their land for speculative property developments. Later, new roads to the north facilitated building in areas such as Marylebone, Camden, Pentonville, Finsbury and Islington. The newly built

Westminster and Blackfriars bridges accelerated development south of the river. Southwark expanded and many Georgian terraces were built in Lambeth, Newington Butts and Kennington. By 1800 90% of London's population were living outside the City boundaries

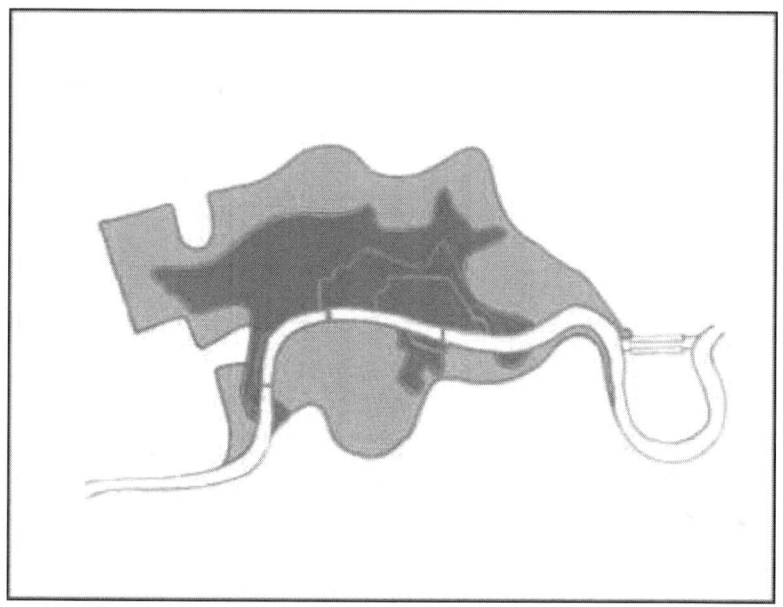

Populated area in 1800 showing the expansion (light grey) since 1700

Nearby villages such as Highgate, Hampstead and Knightsbridge also became popular and housing began to line the main roads connecting them to London. Chelsea, in particular, boomed and the village was linked to Knightsbridge by the Hans Town development involving Sloane Street, Hans Place and finally, in 1790, Cadogan Place. Further out, George III favoured Kew Palace in his later years and grand houses such as Syon House, Kenwood and Osterley were built to Robert Adam designs in rural areas close to London.

Trade and improvement in the transport infrastructure

In this period London became the country's largest manufacturing centre with large factories, mills and breweries as well as small workshops making luxury goods such as clocks, porcelain and furniture. The London silk industry was especially successful based on skilled Huguenot craftsmen in the Spitalfields area.

There was a large increase in trade with the colonies who were required to send their produce to England from where it could be re-exported. The import of sugar was especially profitable, dependent, as it was, on slavery.[49] Port facilities were under great pressure. During the eighteenth century the number of ships docking in London doubled as did the average size of each ship. By the 1790s it could take as long as three months to unload a ship. Warehousing was grossly inadequate and theft was widespread. A shortage of deep water anchorages and dangerous shoals in the Thames meant that insurance costs rocketed adding to the crisis.

While the Howland Great Dock (built in Rotherhithe in 1696 and later forming the core of the Surrey Docks) illustrated the potential of new man-made docks, the City authorities prevaricated. Major expansion in London's docks did not take place until late Georgian times when, to help fund the Napoleonic War, monopolies were sold to different trading companies. This led to the building of the West India Docks[50] (opened in 1802) in the north of the Isle of Dogs, soon followed by the London, East India and Surrey Docks. The new docks had the first bonded warehouses that were protected by high security walls and their own militias.

West India Dock in 1802 from a painting in The Museum of London, Docklands

At the start of the Georgian period crossing the river remained a problem as there was still only one bridge. The medieval London Bridge was a precious asset for the City authorities and business for the watermen was still good. Both opposed the construction of other crossings. Eventually Westminster[51] (1750) and Blackfriars (1769) bridges were built and the houses and shops on London Bridge were demolished in 1760 to ease the flow of traffic. During this period the canal system was also improved to allow goods to be transported to London and thence to export markets. In the late 1760s the Limehouse Cut connected the River Lee with the Thames and in the 1790s the Grand Junction Canal provided a link between the Midlands and the Thames at Brentford (with a branch to Paddington being opened in 1801).

Two cities, the rich and the poor

The middle class expanded under the Hanoverians. As well as merchants there was a growth in men working in financial services, property development and in professions such as medicine and law. Perhaps a third of the population of Georgian London could reasonably be considered as higher or middle class. Life for them was comfortable. Growing literacy, improvements in printing and the popularity of newspapers[52] meant that news became widely available. Art flourished. The rich had their portraits painted and the less affluent bought prints, often of satirical works by William Hogarth. There was a revival in the theatre and actors such as David Garrick and Sarah Siddons became celebrities. A number of pleasure gardens were opened, of which the New Springs Gardens at Vauxhall and Ranelagh Gardens in Chelsea were the most successful. These offered the elite and the middle class the opportunity, for a fee, to promenade, listen to music, dance and socialise, sometimes amorously, outdoors. In 1730 Hyde Park and Kensington Gardens[53] were separated.

The poorer parts of London suffered from chronic poverty and high levels of crime. Death rates, especially for the newly born, were very high. The new port areas of Limehouse and Wapping were gloomy areas with cheap lodging houses and dirty industries. Drunkenness,[54] prostitution and petty crime were rife and parts of the city were notorious for their criminal gangs. Penalties for crime were harsh. The death penalty was applied for even minor crimes and public hangings at Tyburn (today's Marble Arch) took place at regular intervals and drew large crowds. Destitution was a growing problem with the needy being sent to workhouses where inmates worked for long hours on tasks such as spinning yarn and making shoes. Workhouses were overcrowded and conditions in them were appalling. St. Marylebone workhouse, built in 1752, was designed to hold 300 paupers but was holding over a thousand by the 1790s.

The Church of England was unable, or unwilling, to respond to the needs of the poor although non-conformist groups such as John Wesley's Methodists[55] were more sympathetic. The lack of any coordinated authority for governing the suburbs (the insular City of London remained aloof, jealously protecting its own independence and privileges) also limited any secular response to the problems of security, health, drainage and roads. However, despite this, a number of hospitals were founded in the Georgian Age (including Westminster, Guy's and St. George's) and streets became less squalid after legislation in 1762. The Bow Street Runners were established in 1750 as an embryonic police force but they were largely ineffective and it would be almost another century before the Metropolitan Police was formed.

Timeline

	National events	London events
1714	George I crowned, the start of the Hanoverian dynasty	
1720	South Sea Bubble bursts	Burlington House built
1722		Renovation of Kensington Palace commences
1727	George II crowned	
1735		10 Downing Street first used as Prime Minister's residence
1745		Completion of the west towers of Westminster Abbey
1750		Westminster Bridge opened
1752		Mansion House completed
1760	George III crowned	
1763	Treaty of Paris	
1766		Spencer House completed
1769		Blackfriars Bridge opened
1776	Start of American War of Independence	Building of Somerset House commenced
1778		Wesley Chapel built
1780		Gordon Riots
1802		West India Dock opened
1810	The start of the Regency	

Georgian architecture

Church building was reenergised by legislation in 1711 requiring fifty new churches to be built in an attempt to counter the growth in non-conformist worship. The scheme was backed by Queen Anne and the churches became known as Queen Anne Churches. In the event only twelve churches were built.[56] Nicholas Hawksmoor's Christ Church in Spitalfields is perhaps the most imposing (it was certainly the most expensive) as it was built to make a strong statement to the non-conformist Huguenot residents of the area. St. Martin-in-the-Fields is perhaps the finest.

St. Martin-in-the-Field

While in Continental Europe the *Rococo* style became popular, Georgian England was more conservative and there was a reaction against the 'fancies and affectations' of the late Baroque period. There was also a political element to the change in attitude as the Baroque was associated with Rome's Counter-reformation movement and the Hanoverian monarchs were firmly Protestant. Growing interest in Classical studies and architects visiting Italy on 'Grand Tours' led to the formality of the Palladian style coming back into fashion. A number of important secular buildings were built in this style including Burlington House, the 'Old' Treasury, Mansion House, Horse Guards, Spencer House and Somerset House. The Palladian style was also used by William Kent between 1731 and 1735 for rebuilding a large palace in Kew,[57] for Frederick, the estranged son of George II.

After 1760 English architecture entered a phase of stylistic diversity. War with France made travel to Italy difficult and architects such as Robert Adam and his brother John drew more widely on ancient Greek and Etruscan forms, and indeed the Rococo, for inspiration and built in what is now known as the Neo-classical style. Exteriors, while using columns and *friezes*, were less formulaic and the Classical Orders were not adhered to. The Adams most famous development was the Adelphi (Greek for 'brothers') just south of the Strand. While this was demolished in the 1930s, the nearby Royal Society of Arts, Chandos House and buildings in Adam Street illustrate the Adam brothers' style with their extensive use of plaster pilasters, friezes and swags to enliven façades.

Another 'Neo' was also born at this time. Hawksmoor's design for the west towers of Westminster Abbey and George Dance's octagonal nave in St. Bartholomew-the-Less marked the start of the Neo-gothic.

Georgian London

The Georgian period saw the emergence of an increasingly planned approach to urban expansion with the simultaneous construction of whole streets, squares and even of entire districts. This approach was made possible by wealthy families, who owned large tracts of land, using a business model that passed the costs of construction to speculative builders. The area to the north of Oxford Street still resonates with the family names of Grosvenor, Berkley, Burlington, Cavendish, Portman and Harley. Slightly to the east the Bedford family developed Bloomsbury, indeed Bedford Square is the only intact eighteenth-century square remaining in London. Lord North Street and Ely Place are further good examples of Georgian terraces built for the wealthy. Examples of Georgian terrace houses built for the less wealthy remain in Spitalfields including in Elder and Fournier Streets. Building styles were impacted by increased regulation. In particular the 1774 Building Act sought to improve the quality of construction and reduce fire risk. In response architects, increased their use of cast iron for decorative balconies, railings and lamp holders and *Coade stone* was used for decorations.

Bedford Square

Top spots

Bedford Square, WC1	Built between 1775 and 1783, all the buildings in the terraces have five storeys with the main storey, the 'piano nobile', being higher than the others. The door surrounds are made of Coade stone and cast-iron balconies and railings feature prominently. At the centre of the terraces, on each side of the square, the central house is pedimented with Ionic pilasters.
Burlington House, W1	Colen Campbell remodelled the Earl of Burlington's town house in 1720. This was an important move towards the more formal Palladian style of the early Georgian period. The façade of the main building had two storeys with Ionic columns and pilasters.
Chandos House, W1	Built by Robert Adam between 1769 and 17771. The façade is of Craigleith stone, perhaps as an advert for the quarry to the west of Edinburgh on which the Adam brothers had recently taken a lease.
Christ Church, Spitalfields, E1	Designed by Hawksmoor, this large Late Baroque style Queen Anne Church was built between 1714 and 1729. The imposing west front has a large portico, tower and steeple. The interior is 'Wren-like' in everything except its scale. The vast, well lit, interior features five bay aisles with coffered barrel vaults between each pair of *Composite* columns.

Dennis Sever's House, E1	The house is a living museum illustrating the lives of Georgian and Victorian Huguenot silk workers.
Ely Place, EC1	Named after the Bishop of Ely, whose medieval palace once occupied this site, Ely Place is a good example of Georgian terraced housing.
Guildhall, EC2	The present entrance was added in 1788 to replace the decaying medieval porch. Use of a 'Hindoo Gothic' style by George Dance the Younger may have been intended to emphasise London's global importance.
Horse Guards, SW1	The first Horse Guards building was built as part of the Palace of Whitehall in 1664. It was demolished in 1749 and replaced by the current Palladian style guard house designed by William Kent with balustrades and *Palladian windows*. Its attractive octagonal domed clock tower is, however, less obviously Palladian in style.
Jewel Tower, SW1	The late medieval tower was used as a record store in the Georgian period and light was needed. Wren added some rather inelegant round headed windows and Hawksmoor some smaller square headed ones.
Kensington Palace, W8	Between 1722 and 1727 the Jacobean core of Kensington Palace was demolished and replaced by the elaborate Cupola Room, with its coffered ceiling. The King's State Apartments were also remodelled internally by William Kent. The palace was used by George II but not by George III although it was occupied by his son and the future Queen Victoria was born there in 1819.

Georgian London

Lord North Street, SW1	Named after the Prime Minister who presided over the loss of the American colonies, Lord North Street is a good example of Georgian terraced housing.
Mansion House, EC4	Designed by George Dance the Elder in the Palladian style, the Mansion House was built between 1739 and 1752 to be the home of the Lord Mayor. It has three main storeys over a rusticated base. The entrance façade has a portico with six Corinthian columns, approached by a double flight of stairs. The portico has a pediment with a sculpture of a symbolic figure of the City of London trampling on her enemies. Inside, the massive Banqueting Hall is in an Egyptian style.
Museum of London, Docklands, E14	Set in one of the original West India Dock warehouses, the museum deals with the history of the docklands from its construction to its recent regeneration as a centre for financial services.
'Old' Admiralty, SW1	Officially called the Ripley Building, this massive three storey stone and brick building was designed by Thomas Ripley as perhaps London's first purpose-built office building. Completed in 1726, it was initially criticised as being neither Baroque nor Palladian. While most of the building faces onto Horse Guard's Parade it has a high portico supported by Ionic columns facing Whitehall. The impact of this view has, however, been somewhat reduced by a Robert Adam screen, which was added in 1788.

'Old' Treasury, SW1 **ESSENTIAL**	Designed by William Kent and built between 1733 and 1737, this delightfully proportioned building seems rather neglected in a corner of Horse Guards Parade. It is raised on a rusticated basement and has balconies on two floors and a portico supported by four Ionic columns with a splendid coat of arms in its pediment.
Royal Hospital for Seamen, Greenwich, SE10 **ESSENTIAL**	The King William Block contains the Painted Hall with its impressive murals and ceiling painted by James Thornhill between 1707 and 1726. The fine galleried chapel in the Queen Mary Block was destroyed by fire in 1779 and redesigned by James 'Athenian' Stuart in a Greek Revival style with an elaborate ceiling and columns made from *scagliora*.
Royal Society of Arts, WC2	Built in 1774 by John Adam, this fine building with its plaster pilasters, friezes and sags remains the headquarters of the Society for the Encouragement of Arts, Manufactures and Commerce (better known as the Royal Society of Arts).
St. Bartholomew-the-Less, EC1	The octagonal nave with its star-shaped rib vaulting was designed in 1789 by George Dance the Younger. Much of it was however rebuilt in the Victorian period.
St. George's, Hanover Square, W1	Built in 1721, this Queen Anne Church was designed by John James in a late Baroque style. It is not unlike a Wren church although the tower is integrated into the church. It has a fine Grinling Gibbons reredos and sixteenth-century Dutch stained glass.

St. John's, Smith Square, SW1	This Queen Anne Church, built between 1713 and 1728, was designed by Thomas Archer. Each façade of the late Baroque style church is aligned with a street. Its four towers led to it being called 'Queen Anne's footstool'.
St. Luke's, Old Street, EC1	Built in 1733, this Queen Anne Church was designed by John James although the imposing, rather severe, obelisk spire, tower and the flanking wings were by Hawksmoor. Rather disappointingly, here is little to seen in the interior.
St. Martin-in-the-Fields, WC2 **ESSENTIAL**	St. Martin's is another Queen Anne Church built in 1724 to a design by James Gibbs. The west front has a portico with a pediment supported by six Corinthian columns. In designing the church, with its gallery and awe-inspiring ceiling, Gibbs drew upon Wren's work although the tower is integrated.
St Mary-le-Strand, WC2	Commenced in 1714, this Queen Anne Church was designed by James Gibbs, influenced by his recent Grand Tour. Gibbs' Italian Baroque design has a richly decorated coffered plaster ceiling, pilasters behind niches and a columned west front and porch. The steeple however shows the Wren influence.
St. Mary Woolnoth, EC3	The proportions of this imposing late Baroque church are rather unusual and the original woodwork is impressive. Built between 1716 and 1727, this Queen Anne Church is the only Hawksmoor church in the City.

Somerset House, WC2	Originally the site of a Tudor palace, Somerset House was built between 1776 and 1801 to house the Navy Office and for other public activities. It was designed by Sir William Chambers based on old drawings by Inigo Jones.
Spencer House, SW1 **ESSENTIAL**	Built between 1756 and 1766, John Vardy was responsible for the Palladian external elevations with its rusticated ground floor and windows framed by Doric columns. Vardy was however replaced by James 'Athenian' Stuart, then newly returned from Greece. As a result, Spencer House is graced with Greek decoration in the Palm Room and the Great Room. These have recently been splendidly restored.
Wesley Chapel, House and Methodist Museum, EC1	Both the chapel and house are good examples of Georgian buildings built in 1778 to a simple Neo-classical design by George Dance the Younger. Wesley described the chapel as 'neat but not fine' but this was to be changed by Victorian modifications.
Westminster Abbey, SW1	Repairs were made to the north front in the 1720s and the great rose window was restored. Between 1735 and 1745 the towers on the west front (left unfinished from medieval times) were completed by Hawksmoor. These were largely Neo-gothic in style but with Classical flourishes such as the open pediments above the clock face.

Regency London

Overview of the period between 1810 and 1837

The Regency period is generally considered to extend beyond the decade when George III was unable to rule due to insanity to include the reigns of his sons George IV and William IV. George III first suffered apparent attacks of insanity around 1788 and in 1810 his condition became permanent. His son, the future George IV, ruled in his place as Prince Regent between 1811 and 1820. George was very extravagant and grossly self-indulgent. He showed little interest in politics and during this period both the reputation and the power of the monarchy declined. His brother, William IV, was more popular but there was a growing demand for Parliamentary reform and the Great Reform Act was passed in 1832. This led to an expansion of the electoral franchise, the reorganisation of constituencies and the establishment of the elected House of Commons as being the most important branch of Parliament.

The Regency was also a very important period in the physical evolution of modern London both in terms of quantity and quality. In this short period the population of London almost doubled and there was a building boom with areas around Hyde Park and south of the river in Vauxhall and Camberwell being rapidly developed. The Treaty of Vienna in 1815 brought a successful end to the Napoleonic War and Britain was the most powerful country in Europe. The building of the National Gallery, the British Museum, the Wellington Arch and Trafalgar Square demonstrated a strong sense of patriotic pride. There were also a number of improvements to the transport infrastructure. In particular, the Regent Street development improved traffic flows and a new London Bridge and three other new bridges were built across the Thames.

Remodelling the West End

The long war against France had finished and the country was brimming with confidence. George, first as Prince Regent and then as King George IV, commissioned John Nash to undertake a number of developments to demonstrate the Nation's, and more importantly probably his own, importance. Between 1812 and 1820 Regent's Park[58] was landscaped and a number of splendid terraces were built on its periphery. Nash designed a 'Royal Way' to link the new Regent's Park to Pall Mall. Regent Street, as this was called, along with Piccadilly Circus, Waterloo Place and later Trafalgar Square, added grandeur to this part of London as well as providing an important north-south route. Nash was to undertake further commissions for George IV including the costly extensions to Buckingham Palace.

London's population almost doubled in this short period to about 1,900,000. The 1820s saw the development of land to the north and south of Hyde Park. Marshy areas in Belgravia and Pimlico were filled with earth extracted from St. Katherine's Dock and terraces were built by Thomas Cubitt (the first developer to employ his own building workers). To the north of the park, Paddington, Bayswater, Lancaster Gate and North Kensington were developed. New bridges across the Thames encouraged the expansion of Southwark, Vauxhall and Camberwell and the flourishing docks also led to development at Rotherhide and Wapping.

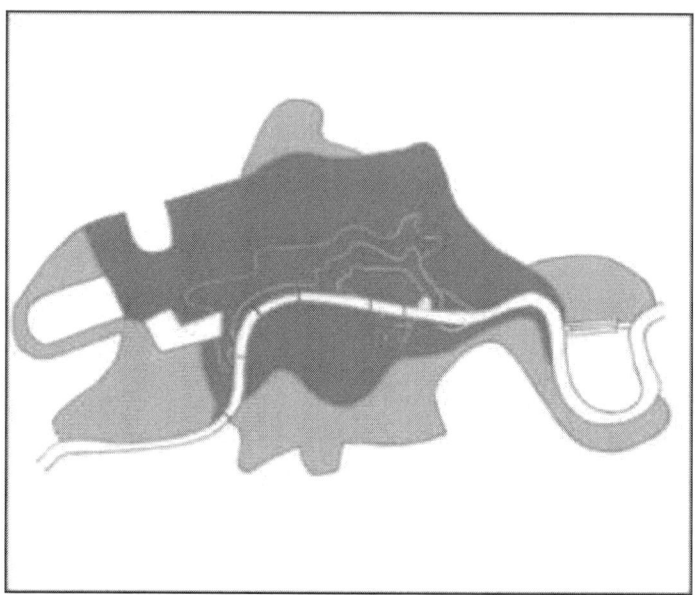

Populated area in 1837 showing the expansion (light grey) since 1800

Trade, banking and retailing

The Industrial Revolution accelerated in the Regency and London started to feel pressure from lower cost manufacturing in the North and the Midlands. However, the city remained an important industrial centre. Shipbuilding was expanded at Millwall and this gave a spur for marine engineering. Leather working in Bermondsey and brewing and distilling in Southwark remained important activities although the silk weavers of Spitalfields suffered from foreign competition.

Great progress was made in financial services and retailing. The Bank of England's monopoly on joint stock banking was withdrawn and new banks were established to help fund the construction of railways and the investment needed to fuel the Industrial Revolution. Large and profitable investments were also made in Europe and America.

Covent Garden market

For the first time a distinct shopping area evolved in London where the wealthy could buy luxury goods. Burlington Arcade, on Piccadilly, opened in 1818 and Oxford, Regent and Bond Streets had many fine shops with large plate glass windows. Gas street lighting appeared in Pall Mall and, by 1823, 40,000 lamps had been installed along 215 miles of London's streets. Some can still be seen today in New Square, EC4. The less attractive large gas holders became part of the London landscape from the 1830s.

101

Improvement to transport infrastructure

There was a spate of bridge building in the Regency and Vauxhall (1816), Waterloo[59] (1817) and Southwark Bridges (1819) were opened - all have subsequently been replaced. The economics of these new bridges, which were privately financed, was linked to property development south of the river and building costs were reduced by the use of cast iron for Vauxhall and Southwark bridges. Around 1820 the decision was made to rebuild London Bridge to improve the Thames' water flow and to ease congestion around the old medieval bridge. The 'new' London Bridge,[60] designed by John Rennie and constructed by his sons, was opened in 1831 at significant cost. An ambitious project to build the Thames Tunnel,[61] the world's first underwater tunnel was also commenced. St Katharine[62] and the West India South Docks were built when the initial monopolies, that had acted as the catalyst for the Georgian docks, expired. The Regent's Canal was completed in 1824 which linked the Paddington Branch of the Grand Junction Canal through Camden to the newly constructed Regent's Canal Dock (now known as the Limehouse Basin).

Timeline

	National events	London events
1810	Start of the Regency	
1815	Treaty of Vienna	
1816		Regent Street commenced, Vauxhall Bridge opened
1817		Waterloo Bridge opened
1818		Burlington Arcade opened
1819		Southwark Bridge opened
1820	George IV crowned	George IV moves to Buckingham Palace
1826		Modifications to Buckingham Palace commenced
1828		Regent Street completed
1829		Metropolitan Police established
1830	William IV crowned	
1831		'New' London Bridge opened
1832	Great Reform Act	Five new constituencies created in London
1834		Palace of Westminster destroyed by fire
1837	Death of William IV	

Regency architecture

As shown by buildings such as the National Gallery, the British Museum and Fishmongers' Hall, Regency secular architecture was largely a continuation of the Neo-classical style. However, Neo-gothic (or as it was called 'Gothic Revival') was often used for church building. In an attempt to keep pace with the rising population (and to address competition from Methodists and Baptists) in 1818, and again in 1824, Parliament approved funding for a massive Anglican church building programme. In the thirty years that followed over one hundred 'Commissioners' Churches'[63] were built in London. Most were either Neo-gothic or Neo-classical in style but some are described as being Norman Revival (for example St. Saviour's, Chelsea) and one is even Byzantine Revival (Christ Church, Streatham). Gothic Revival was also the style chosen for rebuilding the Palace of Westminster after it was burnt down in 1834.[64]

Typical Regency upper or middle class houses were brick covered in *stucco* and with wrought iron balconies and bow windows. Fluted Greek columns and moulded cornices made of stucco, such as those seen in Regent's Square and York Terrace, were also fashionable. The dominance of the terraced house continued and crescents, such as Park Crescent at the top of Portman Place, became popular. However, the middle classes were starting to reject the uniformity of inner-city Georgian housing. Park Village East and Park Village West (just to the north east of Regent's Park) were a response, providing a variety of styles including Gothic Revival villas and semi-detached buildings all with their own gardens. This was to provide an inspiration for later Victorian suburban development.

The National Gallery

Top spots

All Souls, Langham Place, W1	This 'Commissioners' Church' was designed by John Nash and was consecrated in 1824. The idiosyncratic spire is composed of seventeen concave sides supported by a ring of Corinthian columns. Inside, the church is 'Wren-like' with a magnificent feeling of light and space. The church's rotunda was designed to provide an eye-catching monument at the point where Regent Street bends westward to align with the pre-existing Portland Place.
Bank of England, EC2	Between 1788 and 1830 the Bank's interior was remodelled by Sir John Soane to have a number of public banking halls lit by elegant domes. Regrettably these did not survive rebuilding in the 1930s. A surviving feature, albeit modified, is the Tivoli Corner portico (on the corner of Prince's Street and Lothbury). In 1828 Soane built the Neo-classical security wall that also remains today.
British Museum, WC1	Designed by Sir Robert Smirke, this Greek Neo-classical building has a magnificent portico supported by Ionic columns (the *tympanum* sculpture, depicting man's ascent from being a savage, was added in the 1850s). The building took many years to complete. The King's Library on the ground floor, with its towering bookcases and granite columns, was handed over in 1827 but the museum did not fully open to the public until 1857.

Brunel Museum, SE16	A small but very interesting museum is located in the pump house next to the southern shaft that provided access to the Thames Tunnel which ran from Rotherhithe to Wapping.
Buckingham Palace, SW1 **ESSENTIAL**	Originally known as Buckingham House, the building at the core of today's palace was a large town house built for the Duke of Buckingham in 1703. It was acquired by King George III in 1761 as a private residence for Queen Charlotte and became known as the Queen's House. George IV decided to create a new palace. Between 1826 and 1830 John Nash remodelled the interior and created an open forecourt framed by Neo-classical porticos. What is now Marble Arch stood in the centre of the forecourt acting as a grand entrance and the Wellington Arch was also nearby.
Burlington Arcade, W1	Opened in 1818, this was the longest arcade in the country featuring over 50 bow-fronted shops with living space above. The arcade was lit by skylights. To provide variety there were three types of shop unit (single, double and heightened double) and some had doors set at an angle. The Piccadilly Arcade, which is opposite, was built in 1909.
Covent Garden, WC2	The original market, consisting of wooden stalls and sheds, became disorderly and in 1828 the Duke of Bedford commissioned Charles Fowler to design a Neo-classical market building. This involved three parallel store areas enclosed by an arcade of Tuscan columns interspersed at the corners with pyramid-roofed pavilions.

Cumberland Terrace, NW1	Completed in 1826, this is one of several terraces and crescents around Regent's Park designed by John Nash. Intended to stand opposite the proposed summer palace, Cumberland Terrace was of particular importance to the project and is exceptionally grand consisting of three main blocks linked by decorative arches. The central block includes a large sculptured pediment above a long Ionic colonnade.
Dulwich Picture Gallery, SE21	Designed by John Soane, the single storey gallery was opened in 1817. To reduce costs the gallery was built in brick with the expensive Portland stone only used in the lantern, frieze and along the base of the building. To the west, the mausoleum is shaped to recall a funeral monument, with urns, sarcophagi and sacrificial altars in the corners.
Fishmongers' Hall, EC4	The medieval hall was destroyed in the Great Fire and a replacement was demolished to facilitate the construction of the 'new' London Bridge. The current Neo-classical hall opened in 1834.
Lambeth Palace, SE1	The residential part of the medieval palace was demolished and replaced by a Gothic Revival style building designed by Edward Blore. Completed in 1833, the Blore Building as it came to be known, was built in Bath stone which has weathered to be quite yellow. Blore also restored the Guard Room and connected it to the rest of his building. The palace, especially

	the chapel, was badly damaged in the Second World War and has been restored.
Marble Arch, W1	Faced with white marble, this triple arch with Corinthian columns was designed by John Nash in 1827 to be the state entrance of Buckingham Palace. Together with the Wellington Arch it celebrated victory in the Napoleonic Wars. It was relocated in 1851 and again in the early 1960s.
National Gallery, WC2	Designed by William Wilkins and built between 1832 and 1838, the Gallery's Neo-classical design was criticised for being insufficiently grand and its central cupola was unflatteringly described as being like a 'pepper pot'.
Park Crescent, W1	Park Crescent is a semi-circle of elegant stuccoed terraced houses, once either side of Portland Place. Designed by John Nash, the crescent was an integral part of the scheme linking Central London to Regent's Park.
Piccadilly Circus, W1	Piccadilly Circus was created in 1819, at the junction of Piccadilly with the new Regent Street. Initially it was known as Regent's Circus South (Oxford Circus was called Regent's Circus North).
Regent Street, W1	Originally built between 1816 and 1824, Nash's stylish street was rebuilt between 1904 and 1915. The only original building is All Souls Church, Langham Place (see above).
St. Dunstan-in-the-West, EC4	The church was rebuilt in 1830 by John Shaw as an octagonal building with a square tower and octagonal lantern. It is well known for its projecting clock. Inside it has distinctive Lierne

	rib vaulting shaped as a star. Some of the internal fabric and several monuments pre-date the rebuilding of the church. For example, the Flemish wood high altar and reredos date from the seventeenth century.
St. Pancras New Church, NW1	Built between 1819 and 1822, the church was designed by Henry Inwood and his father. Inwood visited Athens and took inspiration from the Erectherion (a temple on the north side of the Acropolis). This is especially evident in the massive portico, the apse and the sculpted female figures (Caryatids) acting as columns to the side entrances of the mausoleum. New materials such as scagliola were used and the Caryatids are hollow made from a modified form of Coade stone with cast iron frames.
Sir John Soane's Museum, WC2	The museum, which was Sir John's London home, comprises three terrace houses that he rebuilt between 1792 and 1824. The white Portland stone façade of the middle house is the most interesting and parts of it could almost be Art Deco in style. It features four medieval corbels taken from Westminster Hall as well as Coade stone sculpted female figures (Caryatids).
Waterloo Place, SW1 **ESSENTIAL**	To the south is Carlton House Terrace comprising two massive buildings with Doric colonnades designed by John Nash. The terrace was built on the site of what was once Carlton House which was demolished in 1824. The Doric theme is continued in the porticos and

	balustrades of the two majestic buildings that flank the middle of Waterloo Place. To the east is the Institute of Directors (originally the United Services Club) designed by Nash in 1828 but later remodelled by Decimus Burton. Opposite is the Athenaeum Club, designed by Burton and completed in 1830. The Athenaeum is decorated with a long blue and white frieze inspired by the Elgin Marbles.
Wellington Arch, W1	The Portland stone Wellington Arch (also known as Constitution Arch) was completed in 1830. Designed by Decimus Burton as an entrance to Buckingham Palace from the Royal Parks, it was moved to its present site in 1883 to ease traffic congestion. It is a single arch with Corinthian columns and a coffered ceiling. In 1846 an over-sized statue of the Duke of Wellington mounted on his horse was placed on top of the arch. In 1912 this was replaced by a sculpture of Nike the goddess of war riding on a chariot.

Victorian London

Overview of the period between 1837 and 1901

After the death of her uncle, William IV, Victoria ruled from 20 June 1837 until her death on 22 January 1901. Her reign lasted for 63 years and seven months, a longer period than any of her predecessors. In Britain, as the Industrial Revolution gathered momentum, this was a period of rapid economic growth and innovation. Britain's coal and its new railways and steamships allowed it to dominate world trade. By 1880 it produced over 40% of manufactured goods, and over a half of the commercial cotton cloth, entering world trade. Growing national prosperity benefitted from peace in Europe although the Crimean War (1853-6) was a notable exception. Aided by the supremacy of its navy Britain aggressively pursued its imperial ambitions, particularly in Asia and Africa. By 1901 Britain had amassed the largest empire in history.

London became the world's financial capital and the epicentre of the British Empire. Grand new public buildings were constructed that expressed the Nation's confidence and there was a flood of church building to reflect its religiosity. London's population more than tripled with much of the growth being accommodated in new suburbs with long roads of terraced housing. Events such as the Great Exhibition (1851) and Queen Victoria's Golden (1877) and Diamond (1897) Jubilees added to London's international prestige. While London's elite and middle classes flourished this was also the time of Oliver Twist and Jack the Ripper. Millions lived in poverty in overcrowded and unsanitary slums. Many died from cholera and respiratory diseases cause by London's infamous 'smog'.

112

New suburbs and a cosmopolitan population

London's population increased from 1.9 million in 1840 to 2.7 million in 1851 to 6.7 million at the end of the century. This astonishing growth was partly self-generated as birth rates remained high and death rates, especially of infants, fell due to improvements in medicine and the water supply. It was also fuelled by inward migration from the countryside, the colonies and poorer parts of Central Europe. In particular, a large Irish population settled in the city, refugees from the Irish potato famine (1845-1849). At one stage, Irish immigrants made up about twenty percent of London's population. Jews from Russia and Poland also fled to Britain escaping persecution. Initially the Jewish community grew in the area between Spitalfields and Whitechapel but, over time, many Jewish families relocated to Hackney.

While areas such as Battersea, Islington, Kensington and Lambeth expanded the greatest growth was in the new suburbs. Living in suburbia, at first a luxury for the middle classes, soon became a necessity and there was massive growth in a ring of suburbs including Camberwell, Fulham, Hampstead and Woolwich. Much of the development in the suburbs involved straight streets of brick terraced 'two-up-two-down' houses. These usually had both front and rear access and small gardens and were provided with gas, water and drainage. Most of the houses within the old City boundaries were demolished and replaced by office blocks and the number of people living there declined from 100,000 to 27,000.

Areas of new housing generally leap-frogged the older areas. Little was done about the millions who continued to live in poverty in overcrowded and unsanitary slums in places like Seven Dials, Holborn and Borough. Some relief was provided by philanthropic organisations and individuals. For example, George Peabody built estates for the poor

113

in Pimlico and Clerkenwell and Sydney Waterlow did the same in North London. However, this only scratched the surface of the problem and the first council housing[65] was not provided until 1890. Education of the masses was also neglected. Some voluntary 'Ragged Schools' were set up in the 1840s but compulsory elementary schooling had to await the 1870 Education Act. Thereafter many 'Board Schools' were located in new three storey red brick buildings often with characteristic Dutch gables.

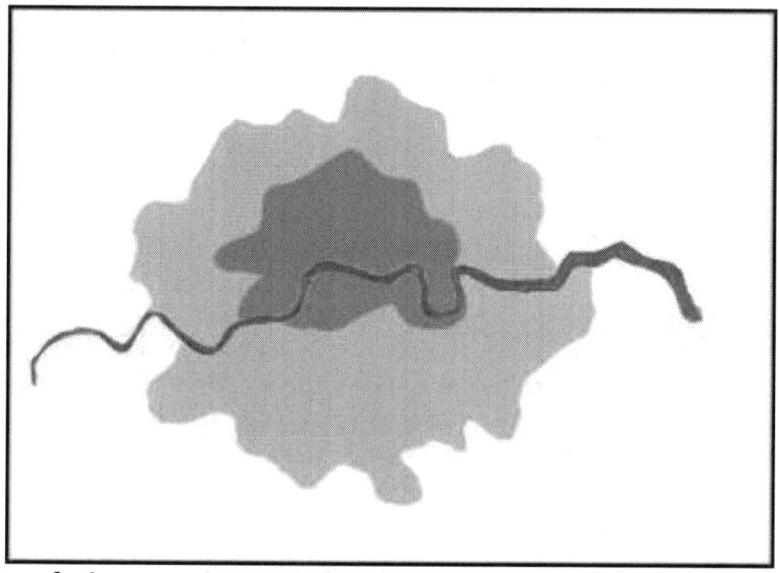

Population area in 1900 showing expansion (light grey) since 1837

Transport improvements

Constructing a national network of railways was one of the most notable achievements of the Victorians. London's very first railway, the London & Greenwich, opened in 1836, travelling at rooftop level over 878 arches. This remains the longest run of brick arches ever built and many still survive in Bermondsey. Services from London reached Bristol and Birmingham in 1838 and fine stations were built at Paddington and, with a massive Neo-classical arch outside it, at Euston.[66] Further links were established to Edinburgh terminating in King's Cross (1852) and to the East Midlands finishing at St. Pancras (1868). Most large termini also had fine hotels such as the Great Western Royal Hotel at Paddington and the Midland Grand Hotel (now the St. Pancras Renaissance Hotel) at St. Pancras. However, building the railways had a devastating impact on some of London's poorer areas and led to the demolition of perhaps 100,000 homes. Neighbourhoods were swept aside to make way for railway tracks, stations and large goods and coal yards. Areas around railway lines soon became associated with urban squalor. In 1846 it was decided that no new surface railways would be allowed to cross the Euston Road from the north.[67] The same rule did not apply to the south and between 1860 and 1866 four railway bridges were constructed across the Thames. With the opening of Blackfriars and Cannon Street stations, commuting from the southern suburbs became easier although still relatively expensive.

Underground trains were one solution to the problem of how to convey passengers from the northern ring of main line stations into Central London. The first subway line in the world, the Metropolitan Line, opened in 1862 linking Paddington and Farringdon. Other lines were soon built, laying the foundations for the modern tube system.[68] London Bridge was widened, and several new road bridges, including Tower Bridge, were opened. Tower Bridge, which opened in 1894, eased congestion and facilitated the development of South East London. Its drawbridge, using innovative hydraulic equipment, allowed shipping to continue to access the Upper Pool of London.

Road transport also improved with the introduction of the horse drawn omnibus, and later horse drawn trams,[69] providing inexpensive forms of passenger transport. Road construction and street widening schemes gradually changed the appearance of central London. New Oxford Street, Clerkenwell Road, Charing Cross Road, Shaftesbury Avenue and Hyde Park Corner were built. Improvements were made to Cannon Street, High Holborn and Kensington High Street and the Holborn Viaduct was constructed. The Victoria, Chelsea and Albert Embankments were also built as part of the creation of London's new Main Drainage System. As well as shielding the sewers these embankments provided new roads and public gardens, facilitated the building of part of the underground system and improved the flow of the Thames thereby reducing the risk of flooding.

Trade, docks and banking

The repeal of the Corn Laws in 1846, saw the end of tariff protection for British agriculture. As a result there was significant growth in the volume of imported food in the 1850s including North American grain, Argentinian beef, Australian mutton and New Zealand lamb. While free trade caused distress in rural areas it led to more business for London. There was further expansion of the docks with the construction of the Royal Victoria (1855), Millwall (1868), Royal Albert (1880) and Tilbury (1886) Docks. Most dock work was poorly paid and casual. These poor working conditions led to militancy and triggered the London dock strike of 1889.[70] The strike helped to draw attention to the problem of poverty in Victorian England and the dockers' cause attracted considerable public sympathy. It also led to the establishment of one of the first trade unions.

The Beckton Gas Works[71] was opened in 1870 by the Gas Light and Coke Company. It manufactured gas for most of London north of the Thames, with numerous older works being closed. Its counterpart south of the river was the East Greenwich Gas Works on the Greenwich Peninsula. The ready availability of coke and gas encouraged the location of activities such as tar distilling and the production of sulphuric acid. Locations such as Silvertown and West Ham became major centres for the British chemical industry. There was, however, a decline in ship building despite Brunel's Great Eastern (launched in 1858) being built at Millwall.

Company law evolved rapidly during the Victorian period facilitating the expansion of business. In particular the legal restrictions around incorporation were relaxed and limited liability introduced. These developments provided opportunities for accountants[72] and the origins of today's large accounting firms can be traced back to this period. The Institute of Chartered Accountants in England and Wales was formed in 1880 and their impressive Chartered Accountants' Hall was opened in 1893 by its president, Edwin Waterhouse.

The increase in corporate activity also led to an increase in demand for banking services. In the eighteenth century banking was mostly undertaken by the Bank of England and a number of relatively small private banks. This was to change in the Regency and Victorian periods. Banks were allowed to limit their liability and many private banks converted to being joint stock companies. In 1854 banks were allowed to enter the clearing system and this was to dramatically increase the use of cheques. Private regional banks rushed to obtain a London presence and many did so by merging with London banks.[73]

More centralised planning

Outside the City of London, governance involved ancient parishes working, or rather not working, alongside a vast array of single purpose boards, commissions and authorities. With London's rapid growth there became an urgent need to reform its system of governance. In an attempt to improve decision making the Metropolitan Board of Works (MBW) was created in 1855. The aim was to provide London, outside the 'Sqaure Mile', with an adequate infrastructure and address issues such as traffic congestion, poor public health and gas companies (presumably most notably the Gas Light and Coke Company) from abusing their monopoly powers. Initially the MBW was given responsibility for sewage, roads and public spaces. Later additional responsibilities included the fire brigade (in response to the Tooley Street fire[74] of 1861), tramways and bridges. It also administered the Building Act and saved areas such as Hampstead Heath, Clapham Common and Blackheath from development. Importantly the MBW was not given responsibility for improving housing and many of the poor still lived in warrens of damp one-roomed dwellings with only primitive sanitation. The City of London was not involved in these reforms. It retained its ancient customs and resisted all attempts to expand its responsibilities to encompass the wider urban area.

Dealing with London's sewerage was one of the MBW's great successes. In the middle of the century raw sewage was pumped straight into the Thames and this culminated in what was known as the 'Great Stink' of 1858. Polluted drinking water (sourced from the Thames) also brought diseases such as typhoid and cholera[75] to London's population. Parliament finally gave consent for the MBW to construct a massive system of sewers. The Main Drainage System[76] was completed in 1875. The engineer in charge of building the new system, and many of the other important London construction projects of the time, was Joseph Bazalgette.

Members of the MBW were appointed not elected. Over time this lack of a democratic foundation made it unpopular with Londoners and in 1888 it was replaced with the directly elected London County Council (LCC). Initially the LCC covered the same geographical area and had the same responsibilities as the MBW although the area it covered was now designated as the 'County of London'. Westminster was transferred to it from Middlesex in 1889 and in 1900, the County was sub-divided into 28 metropolitan boroughs to further improve the degree of local accountability. In 1904, the LCC took over responsibility for education.

Timeline

	National events	London events
1837	Victoria crowned	
1843		Thames Tunnel completed
1844		Trafalgar Square completed
1846		Waterloo Station opened
1851		Great Exhibition
1853	Crimea War starts	
1855		The Metropolitan Board of Works formed
1856		Completion of Buckingham Palace
1858		The 'Great Stink'
1861	Death of Prince Albert	Tooley Street Fire.
1862		A new Westminster Bridge and the first underground line opened
1869		Blackfriars Bridge and Holborn Viaduct opened on the same day
1870		Completion of the Palace of Westminster
1872		The Albert Memorial built
1875		Completion of the Main Drainage System
1884		Circle Line completed
1888		London County Council formed
1889		London dock strike
1894		Tower Bridge opened
1901	Death of Queen Victoria	

Victorian architecture

The Neo-classical style remained popular throughout the nineteenth century and was used for many secular buildings such as the Albert Hall, the Natural History Museum, the Royal Exchange and Smithfield Market as well as new offices in Whitehall[77] built to house a growing bureaucracy.

The Royal Exchange

However, the Victorian period is best remembered for the Neo-gothic style favoured by Augustus Pugin, who considered Gothic 'the only

Christian style'. The 'Gothic Revival', as it was termed, reflected a romantic yearning for the Middle Ages. This nostalgia may, in part, have been a reaction to the Industrial Revolution. Examples of the Neo-gothic style are seen in many of the churches, the Palace of Westminster, the Albert Memorial and the Royal Courts of Justice.

Royal Courts of Justice

Many of London's suburban churches date from the Victorian period. Initially this was a continuation of the 1818 Commissioners' Church programme but, as Evangelical activism increased and there was a revival in Anglo-Catholicism, many new churches were constructed and many old ones enlarged and 'modernised' by stripping out galleries and box pews. Architects such as George Gilbert Scott, George Street and John Loughborough Pearson were especially active. Influenced by Pugin, most of the new churches were in the Gothic style but there was innovation in the use of building materials. Bricks of different colours (polychromy) were used and there was innovative use of stained glass, metalwork and ceramics. As shown by St. Cuthbert's, Philbeach Gardens and Holy Trinity, Sloane Street, the Arts and Crafts movement was to become popular after 1880. All Saints, Margaret Street and the church of St. James-the-Less, in Pimlico, provided a foretaste of this.

Around 1870 there was a reaction against 'pure' Gothic and Classical styles for domestic architecture and the two were combined as they had been in seventeenth-century Dutch architecture. Richard Norman Shaw's Alliance Assurance Office in St. James' illustrates this Queen Anne Revival style and it was also used extensively for building new mansion blocks such as those close to the Albert Hall.

While most Victorian architecture is 'Neo' of one form or another there was innovation with the use of new materials and styles. Iron and later steel were used to provide building skeletons and beams became lighter and stronger after the invention of the 'I' girder in the 1840s. Tower Bridge, while largely steel, is cased in stone thereby providing an extreme example of Neo-gothic architecture. Examples of the visible use of metal are the main railway stations, Holborn Viaduct and Smithfield Market. Naval dockyard and greenhouse buildings provided the basis for other innovative constructions solely of glass and iron. The Palm House in Kew Gardens was constructed between 1846 and 1848, and perhaps the finest example was the Crystal Palace built by Joseph Paxton for the Great Exhibition in 1851[78] and destroyed by fire in 1936.

Smithfield Market

Top spots

Albert Hall, SW7	Opened in 1871, the Neo-classical design was inspired by Roman amphitheatres. It was constructed mainly of red brick, with terracotta decoration. The dome on top was made of wrought iron. Nearby mansion blocks, such as Albert Hall Mansions designed by Richard Norman Shaw, illustrate the Queen Anne Revival style that became popular after 1870.
Albert Memorial, W2	This Neo-gothic memorial was commissioned by Queen Victoria in memory of her beloved husband, Prince Albert, who died of typhoid in 1861. Designed by Sir George Gilbert Scott, the Memorial has an ornate canopy containing a statue of the prince.
All Saints, Margaret Street, W1	Built between 1850 and 1859, this Anglo-Catholic church was designed by William Butterfield. The exterior was innovative with the use of three colours of brick and the tall pointed spire being banded with stone. The interior is richly patterned with inlays of marble and tile. The polychrome pulpit is similar to that at St. James-the-Less. The north wall is dominated by a large ceramic tile frieze depicting figures from the Old Testament.
Alliance Assurance Office, SW1	Designed by Richard Norman Shaw in the Queen Anne Revival style this building, which opened in 1883, provided a novel mixture of offices and flats.

Buckingham Palace, SW1	Victoria and Albert found the palace too small and commissioned Edward Blore to design a new wing facing the Mall. This involved enclosing Nash's forecourt and necessitated moving Marble Arch. Blore created the central portico with its famous first floor balcony. The façade of the east wing was remodelled again in 1913 and the three prominent porticos seen today date from this period.
Burlington House, W1	Originally built in the Palladian style, Burlington House was taken over by the Royal Academy in 1867 and modifications were required. Sidney Smirke sympathetically added a third storey to the central building with statues in niches and Palladian windows. The east and west wings were also replaced with larger versions and the gateway onto Piccadilly was reconstructed in its current coffered round arched style.
Charing Cross, WC2	Edward I had a number of Eleanor Crosses built between 1291 and 1294 to mark the route of the passage of his dead queen from Lincoln to London. Two were in London but were destroyed in the Civil War. A Victorian replica of the most elaborate stands today outside Charing Cross station. It is an extraordinarily ornate Neo-gothic memorial with a number of niches containing statues.
Chartered Accountants' Hall, EC2	Designed by John Belcher in an ornate Neo-baroque style, the hall was opened in 1893. The entrance porch has two Tuscan columns supporting a fine open scrolled pediment and

	there is much statutory on the exterior. Inside, the former Council Chamber is impressive and the former library, entrance hall and main staircase are especially noteworthy.
Covent Garden, WC2	Fowler's Regency market was largely open air. In 1874 William Cubitt added roofs and, over time, the Floral Hall and Charter Market were added. In 1904 the Jubilee Market for foreign flowers was built.
Foreign and Commonwealth Office, SW1	Designed by George Gilbert Scott, construction on this Neo-classical building began in 1861 and finished in 1868. Built to impress dignitaries from other countries it has a grand staircase and ornate reception rooms decorated with marble, murals and ornately carved ceilings.
Gibson Hall, EC2	This Neo-classical building with its curved façade and paired Composite columns was designed by John Gibson in 1862 for the National Provincial Bank. It is decorated with carved panels and statues symbolising the industries and crafts for which the Bank supplied finance. The entrance is roofed with a barrel vault.
Holborn Viaduct, EC1	The viaduct was built between 1863 and 1869 to improve road links between the City and the West End. Four pavilions contain staircases down to Farringdon Street below. The parapets are adorned with statutes representing commerce and agriculture (on the south side) and science and fine arts (on the north side). There are also statues of Lord

	Mayors William Walworth and Henry Fitz-Ailwin.
Holy Trinity, Sloane Street, SW1	Built in the Gothic Revival style to a design by John Dando Sedding this, the widest of London's churches, is a testament to the Arts and Crafts movement. The interior has elaborate carvings and plaster work, naturalistic wrought iron chancel gates and unusual choir stalls. The stained glass is magnificent, especially the enormous east window by Edward Burne-Jones and William Morris.
Leadenhall Market, EC3	Designed in 1881 by Sir Horace Jones (who was also the architect of Billingsgate and Smithfield Markets), the market is notable for its ornate roof structure (painted green, maroon and cream) and its cobbled floors.
Lloyd's Registry Building, EC3 **ESSENTIAL**	Completed in 1901, Thomas Collcutt's inventive design uses first-class materials both inside and out. Portland stone and grey limestone were used on the façades and marble, oak and mahogany used for doors, skirting and floors. Many ceilings are richly decorated with Renaissance style paintings in tempera. While largely Neo-classical, the building has hints of Gothic and even Art Deco.
National Gallery, WC2	Landscaping of Trafalgar Square and, in particular the creation of the northern terrace, improved the appearance of the Gallery. The internal space was improved by the addition of the Charles Barry wing in 1876.

Natural History Museum, SW7 **ESSENTIAL**	The museum was mostly designed by Alfred Waterhouse in his own idiosyncratic Neo-classical style. Work began in 1873 and the new museum opened in 1881. Both the interiors and exteriors of the building make extensive use of terracotta tiles and there are many relief sculptures of flora and fauna.
Paddington Station, W2	The main station, designed by Isambard Kingdom Brunel, was opened in 1854. The glazed roof is supported by wrought iron arches.
Palace of Westminster, SW1 **ESSENTIAL**	Following the 1834 fire, construction of the replacement Neo-gothic Parliament building started in 1840 and lasted for 30 years. Charles Barry's design made extensive use of iron girders cloaked in stone. The young Augustus Pugin, a great enthusiast of Gothic architecture, assisted Barry and designed much of the interior and what is now known as the Elizabeth Tower (more commonly 'Big Ben'). The St. Stephen's Hall, the octagonal Central Lobby and the House of Lords (containing the monarch's throne and canopy) are especially spectacular. In contrast, the chamber of the House of Commons is relatively sombre with its dark wood ceiling and wall panelling.
Piccadilly Circus, W1	The circus lost its circular form in 1886 with the construction of Shaftesbury Avenue. The statue of Eros was added in 1893 as a memorial to Lord Shaftesbury.

Royal Courts of Justice, WC2 **ESSENTIAL**	Designed by George Edmund Street, the courts were opened by Queen Victoria in 1882. The Strand facing side is perhaps the most fanciful of London's Neo-gothic buildings with a variety of towers, turrets (tourelles), slender spires (fleches), arches and windows. The other sides are less flamboyant but the red brick is enlivened by stone banding and chequered work.
Royal Exchange, EC3	Opened in 1844, the third Royal Exchange building (the previous two having been destroyed by fire) was designed by William Tite as a four-sided structure surrounding a central courtyard. The internal works made use of concrete and cast iron. Externally, as well as the imposing Classical Corinthian portico, there is a mixture of architectural styles including Baroque and French Second Empire.
St. Augustine's, Kilburn, NW6	Built in 1871 to inspire London's Irish Catholic community, this is a shining example of Victorian Gothic Revival architecture. Designed by John Loughborough Pearson, the size and ornateness of this stunning red brick structure has led to it being called the 'Cathedral of North London'. Exterior features include a tall spire and an elaborate west front with a large rose window. Inside, each side has arcaded aisles with galleries that cross the transept like bridges.

St. Cuthbert's, Philbeach Gardens, SW5	Designed by Hugh Roumieu Gough, this Anglo-Catholic church was completed in 1887 and is today a shrine to the Arts and Crafts movement. Built of brick, with stone dressing, its Decorated Gothic style recalls the monastic churches of the Middle Ages. Its fine metal work includes the rood screen, the lectern and a most unusual clock. The vast wooden reredos was designed by Ernest Geldart.
St. James-the-Less, Pimlico, SW1	Designed by George Edmund Street, the church was built between 1858 and 1861. The red brick exterior is Neo-gothic, inside, however, there is a foretaste of the Arts and Crafts movement in the pulpit, the multi coloured tiling and the stained glass windows. The colourful fresco by George Watts is especially delightful.
St. Mary Magdalene, Paddington, W2	The church was designed by George Street, in the Gothic Revival style. Work started in 1865 but, although completed in 1872, a fire destroyed the brand-new roof so the first Mass could not be celebrated until the following year. The walls of the chancel are covered with alabaster panels and mosaics and the crypt recreates a medieval Catholic sanctuary chapel.
St. Pancras Station, N1 **ESSENTIAL**	George Gilbert Scott's Neo-gothic brick station was completed in 1868. 23 wrought iron arches, proudly proclaiming to be made in Derbyshire, carry a massive glass roof across six platforms. The four storey St. Pancras Renaissance Hotel (previously the Midland

	Grand Hotel) was completed in 1873. The brick façade is a fantastic assembly of pointed windows, arches and arcading. The skyline is an especially interesting concoction of towers, turrets, spires, chimneys and gables – Walt Disney could not have done better! The entrance hall (now a bar) is a lavish display of coloured stone, gilded carving and stencilled patterns and there is a fine staircase.
Smithfield Market, EC1	Completed in 1868, Smithfield Market was designed by Sir Horace Jones using both prefabricated cast and wrought iron. The central road (Grand Avenue) is spanned by cast iron frames with fine filigree decoration. Octagonal towers with copper domes mark the corners.
Somerset House, WC2	Today's internal courtyard was created by the addition of wings to the east (1831) and west (1856) designed in the same Palladian style as the main Georgian building.
Tower Bridge, SE1	Tower Bridge, a combined bascule and suspension bridge, was built between 1886 and 1894. Designed by Horace Jones, over 11,000 tons of steel provided the framework for the towers and walkways. The metal was then clad in Cornish granite and Portland stone in a Neo-gothic style.
Tower of London, EC3	Concerned about the possibility of revolution, the Tower of London was strengthened and, in 1845, the massive Neo-gothic sandstone Waterloo Barracks (now the Jewel House) was constructed on the location of a storehouse

	that had been destroyed by a fire. The need for a military presence in Central London is also shown by the construction of the Finsbury Barracks, City Road in 1857.
Trafalgar Square, WC2	This area was previously the King's Mews. In 1826, after the mews were moved to Buckingham Palace, redevelopment commenced based on John Nash designs. Progress was slow and the square did not open until 1844. The Corinthian Nelson's Column was constructed between 1840 and 1843.
Wesley Chapel, House and Methodist Museum, EC1	The simplicity of Wesley's original chapel was to be dramatically changed by the addition of marble columns, a reredos and stained glass windows. Additional wings were also built, one of which has a fine glass roof with wooden surround. A special treat is the gentlemen's toilets in the basement dating back to 1891.
Westminster Abbey, SW1	The high altar and reredos were remodelled by George Gilbert Scott in 1867 and, in the 1880s, Scott and J.L. Pearson restored the North Transept and redesigned the rose window.
Westminster Bridge, SE1	By the mid-1800s the Georgian bridge was subsiding badly and needed replacement. The new bridge, which opened in 1862, is the oldest remaining road bridge across the Thames in Central London. The seven arch wrought iron bridge was designed by Thomas Page and some of the Neo-gothic detail was provided by Charles Barry.

London 'Top spots' by post code

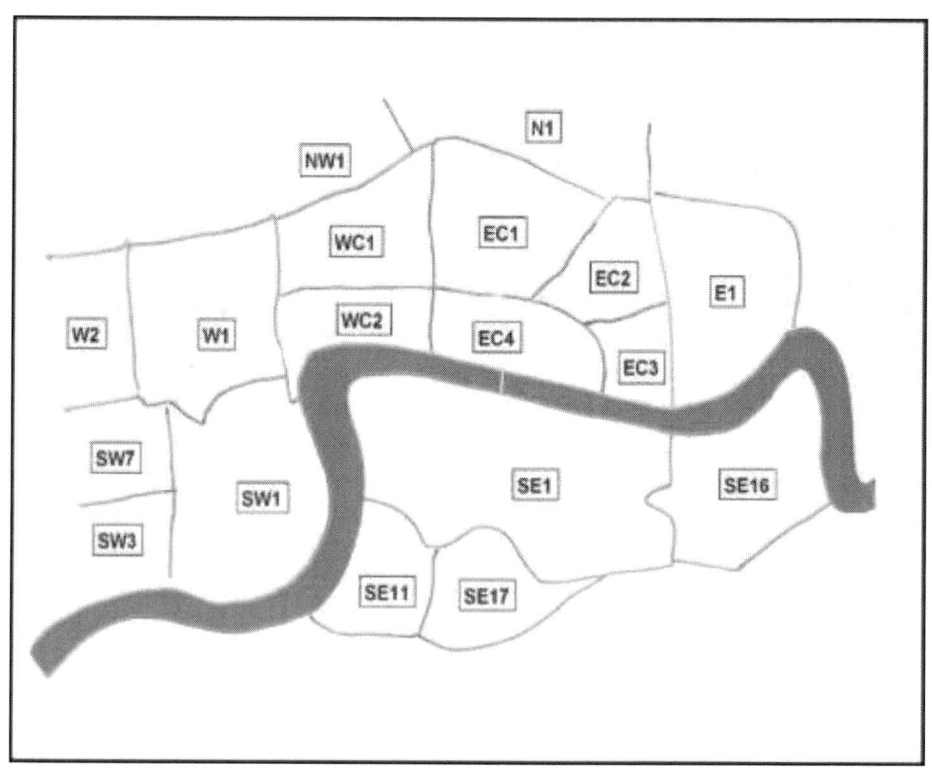

Central London post codes

'Top spot'	Page	Address
South West		
SW1		
Alliance Assurance Office	125	1 St. James' Street, SW1A 1EF
Banqueting House	72	Whitehall, SW1A 2ER. Historic Royal Palaces. Entrance fee.
Buckingham Palace	107, 126	Spur Road, SW1A 1AA
Foreign and Commonwealth Office	127	King Charles Street, SW1A 2AH
Holy Trinity, Sloane Street	128	146 Sloane Street, SW1X 9BZ
Horse Guards	93	Whitehall, SW1A 2AX
Jewel Tower	41, 93	Abingdon Street, SW1P 3JX. English Heritage. Entrance fee.
Lord North Street	94	Lord North Street, SW1P
'Old' Admiralty	94	26 Whitehall, SW1A 2PA
'Old' Treasury	95	Next to Horse Guards, Whitehall, SW1A 2AX
Palace of Westminster	25, 43, 129	Parliament Square, London SW1A 0AA. Entrance fee charged.
Queen Anne's Gate	74	Queen Anne's Gate, SW1H 9BT
St. James' Palace	57	Marlborough Road, SW1A 1BS. Not generally open to the public.
St. James-the-Less, Pimlico	131	Vauxhall Bridge Road, Pimlico, SW1V 2PS

St. John's, Smith Square	96	Smith Square, SW1P 3HA
St. Margaret's, Westminster	58	St. Margaret Street, SW1P 3JX
Spencer House	97	27 St. James' Place, SW1A 1NR
Westminster Abbey	26, 46, 59, 97, 133	Victoria Street, SW1P 3PA. Entrance fee. The Chapter House and Pyx Chamber are English Heritage and separate access to them is possible through Dean's Yard.
Waterloo Place	110	Waterloo Place, SW1Y 5ER
SW3		
Chelsea Old Church	56	Old Church Street, London SW3 5DQ
Royal Hospital, Chelsea	74	Royal Hospital Road, Chelsea, SW3 4SR
SW5		
St. Cuthbert's, Philbeach Gardens	131	Philbeach Gardens, SW5 9EB. Limited access.
SW7		
Albert Hall	125	Kensington Gore, SW7 2AP
Natural History Museum	129	Cromwell Road, SW7 5BD

London 'Top spots' by post code

West End		
W1		
All Souls, Langham Place	106	2 All Souls Place, W1B 3DA
All Saints, Margaret Street	125	7 Margaret Street, W1W 8JG
Burlington Arcade	107	51 Piccadilly, W1J 0QJ
Burlington House	92, 126	Piccadilly, W1J 0BA. Free tours take place most days at noon.
Chandos House	92	2 Queen Anne Street, W1G 9LQ
Marble Arch	109	1 Marble Arch, W1H 7DX
Park Crescent	109	Park Crescent, W1B 1PQ
Piccadilly Circus	109, 129	Piccadilly Circus, W1J 9HP
Regent Street	109	Regent Street, W1B 5TD
St. George's, Hanover Square	95	Hanover Square W1S 1FX
Wellington Arch	111	Hyde Park Corner, W1J 7JZ. English Heritage. Entrance fee.
W2		
Albert Memorial	125	Albert Memorial Road, W2 2UH
Paddington Station	129	Praed Street, W2 1AE
St. Mary Magdalene, Paddington	131	Rowington Close, W2 5TF
WC1		
Bedford Square	92	Bedford Square, WC1B 3HH
British Museum	106	Great Russell Street, WC1B 3DG

Staple Inn Chambers	58	7 Grays Inn Road, WC1V 7QH
WC2		
Charing Cross	126	Charing Cross station, the Strand, WC2 5HS
Covent Garden	72, 107, 127	Covent Garden, WC2E 8RF
Lincoln's Inn Chapel	73	Chancery Lane, WC2A 3TJ
National Gallery	109, 128	Trafalgar Square, WC2N 5DN
Royal Courts of Justice	129	The Strand, WC2A 2LL
Royal Society of Arts	95	8 John Adam Street, WC2N 6EZ
St. Clement Danes	75	The Strand, WC2R 1DH
St. Mary-le-Strand	96	The Strand, WC2R 1ES. Limited access.
St. Martin-in-the-Fields	58, 96	Trafalgar Square, WC2N 4JJ
St. Paul's, Covent Garden	78	Covent Garden, WC2E 8RF
Sir John Soane's Museum	110	13 Lincoln Inn Fields, WC2A 3BP.
Somerset House	97, 132	The Strand, WC2R 1LA
Trafalgar Square	133	Trafalgar Square, WC2N 5DN
York House Watergate	79	Thames Embankment Gardens, WC2
W8		
Kensington Palace	73, 93	Kensington Gardens, W8 4PX. Historic Royal Palaces. Entrance fee.
W14		
Holland House	73	Abbotsbury Road, Kensington, W14 8EL

Eastern Central

EC1		
Charterhouse	41, 56, 72	38 Charterhouse Street, EC1M 6JH. The chapel and a small museum are free. Entrance fee charged for a tour of the rest of the property.
Ely Place	93	Ely Place, EC1N 6RY
Holborn Viaduct	127	Holborn Viaduct, EC1A
St. John's Gate	58	St. John's Lane, Clerkenwell, EC1M 4DA. It contains the museum of the Order of St. John which is free entry.
Priory Church of St. John	43	St. John's Lane, Clerkenwell, EC1M 4DA. Only open Tuesday, Friday and Saturday,11am and 2.30pm (tours last 80 minutes)
St. Bartholomew-the-Great	25, 57	West Smithfield, EC1A 9DS (outside the hospital area). Entrance fee.
St. Bartholomew-the-Less	43, 95	West Smithfield, EC1A 7BE (within the hospital area)
St. Luke's, Old Street	96	Old Street, EC1V 9NG
Smithfield Market	132	West Smithfield, EC1A 9PS
Wesley Chapel, House and Methodist Museum	97, 133	49 City Road, EC1Y 1AU. Open every week day free of charge. Once a month there is an open house with very helpful guides.

EC2		
Bank of England	106	Threadneedle Street, EC2R 8AH A free of charge museum can be accessed from Bartholomew Lane.
Chartered Accountants' Hall	126	1 Moorgate Place, EC2R 6AE
Guildhall	41, 93	Gresham Street, EC2 7HH
Gibson Hall	127	13 Bishopsgate, EC2N3BA
London Wall	42	Noble Street, EC2V 7EE
Merchant Taylors' Hall	42	30 Threadneedle Street, EC2R 8JB. While not open to the public, access can sometimes be arranged through the Beadle.
Museum of London	16, 42, 73	150 London Wall, EC2Y 5HN
Roman Amphitheatre	16	Guildhall Art Gallery, Gresham Street, EC2 7HH
St. Ethelburga's	44	78 Bishopsgate, EC2N 4AG
St. Margaret's, Lothbury	76	Lothbury, EC2R 7HH
St. Mary-le-Bow	25	Cheapside, EC2V 6AU
EC3		
All Hallows-by-the-Tower	16, 25	Byward Street, EC3R 5BJ
Leadenhall Market	128	Gracechurch Street, EC3V 1LT
Lloyd's Registry Building	128	71 Fenchurch Street, EC3M 4BS. Interior not open to the

		public but private viewings can be arranged.
Roman Wall	16	Just outside Tower Hill underground station, EC3N 4DJ
Royal Exchange	130	Cornhill, EC3V 3LN
St. Andrew Undershaft	57	St. Mary Axe, EC3A 6AT
St. Helen's	44	St. Helen's Place, EC3A 6AT
St. Katherine Cree	75	85 Leadenhall Street, EC3A 3BP
St. Magnus-the-Martyr	44, 76	Lower Thames Street, EC3R 6DN
St. Mary Woolnoth	96	Lombard Street, EC3V 9EA
The Monument	79	Fish Street Hill, EC3A 8AH. Entrance fee.
Tower of London	26, 45, 59, 132	Tower Hill, EC3N 4AB. Historic Royal Palaces. Entrance fee.
EC4		
London Mithraeum Bloomberg	16	12 Walbrook, EC4 8AA. Entry is free but a booking needs to be made through the Mithraeum website.
Fishmongers' Hall	108	London Bridge, EC4R 9EL
Mansion House	94	Poultry, London EC4N 8BH
Middle Temple Hall	56	Middle Hall Lane, EC4Y 9AT. Open most mornings, Monday to Friday.
Old Cock Tavern, Fleet Street	57	17 Fleet Street, EC4A 2AT
St. Bride's	75	Fleet Street, EC4Y 8AU

St. Dunstan-in-the-West	109	186 Fleet Street, EC4A 2HR
St. Martin-within-Ludgate	76	40 Ludgate Hill, EC4M 7DE
St. Mary Abchurch	77	Abchurch Lane, EC4N 7BA
St. Mary Aldermary	77	Watling Street, EC4M 9BW
St. Paul's Cathedral	77	St. Paul's Churchyard, EC4M 8AD. Entrance fee.
St. Stephen's Walbrook	78	39 Walbrook, EC4N 8BN
Temple Bar Arch	78	Paternoster Square, EC4M 7DX
Temple Church	25, 45	Temple, EC4Y 7BB
Ye Olde Cheshire Cheese	79	145 Fleet Street, EC4A 2BU
South East		
SE1		
George Inn	72	77 Borough High Street, SE1 1NH
Globe Theatre	56	21 New Globe Walk, Bankside, SE1 9DT
Lambeth Palace	42, 56, 73, 108	Lambeth Palace Road, SE1 7JU. Tickets need to be booked in advance. Entrance fee.
Southwark Cathedral	44	London Bridge, SE1 9DA
Tower Bridge	132	Tower Bridge Road, SE1 2UP. Entrance fee.
Westminster Bridge	133	
Winchester Palace	46	Clink Street, SE1 9DA

London 'Top spots' by post code

SE9		
Eltham Palace	41	Court Road, Eltham, SE9 5QA. English Heritage. Entrance fee.
SE10		
Queen's House, Greenwich	74	Romney Road, Greenwich, SE10 9NF
Royal Hospital for Seamen, Greenwich	74, 95	King William Walk, Greenwich, SE10 9NN
SE16		
Brunel Museum	107	Railway Avenue, Rotherhithe, SE16 4LF. Entrance fee.
SE21		
Dulwich Picture Gallery	108	Gallery Road, Dulwich SE21 7AD. Entrance fee.
East		
E1		
Christ Church, Spitalfields	92	Fournier Street, E1 6QE
Dennis Sever's House, Spitalfields	93	18 Folgate Street, Spitalfields, E1 6BX. Open on alternate days, often just for evening tours. Entrance fee.
E9		
Sutton House	58	2 Homerton High Street, Hackney. E9 6JQ. National Trust. Entrance fee.

London 'Top spots' by post code

E14		
Museum of London, Docklands	94	West India Quay, London E14 4AL
North		
N1		
St. Pancras Station	131	Euston Road, N1C 4QP
NW1		
Cumberland Terrace	108	Cumberland Terrace NW1 4HP
St. Pancras New Church	110	Euston Road, NW1 2BA (opposite Euston Station)
NW6		
St. Augustine's, Kilburn	130	Kilburn Park Road, NW6 5XB. Limited access

Glossary of terms

Aisle	In church architecture, an aisle is a passageway to either side of the nave usually divided off by an arcade. In Gothic architecture, the aisle roof is often lower than that of the nave, allowing light to enter through clerestory windows.
Apse	The semi-circular east end of the chancel.
Arcade	A succession of arches, each counter-thrusting the next, supported by columns or piers. Also, a covered walkway supported by a line of arches.
Arch-braced roof	An early form of hammer-beam roof where the rafters are supported by a pair of arch braces.
Architrave	A horizontal decorative moulding, usually the lowest component of an entablature. Also, the moulded frame around a door or window.
Basilica	A Roman public building containing law courts and where important official functions were undertaken.

145

Barrel vaulting

A barrel vault is the simplest of vaults where the roof, shaped like a half cylinder, is directly supported by the walls. A feature of Saxon and Norman Romanesque architecture, a good example is the Chapel of St. Francis of Assisi in the crypt of All Hallows-by-the-Tower.

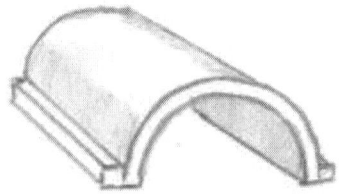

Bay

An architectural division usually the width of an arch.

Blank arcading

A series of arches applied to the surface of a wall as a decorative element. Blank (or blind) arcading commenced with Romanesque architecture and continued to be common in later styles.

Boss

A knob at the central intersection of roof vault ribs. Carved bosses were a common feature in Gothic architecture and good examples can be seen in the ceiling of the undercroft of Lincoln's Inn Chapel.

Burgh

A Saxon fortified settlement. Alfred the Great developed a network of burghs, first in the West Country and then elsewhere, as part of his long campaign to regain England from the Vikings. Inhabitants were granted a degree of autonomy as an incentive for maintenance and manning the defensive walls.

Buttress

A mass of masonry built against a wall to reinforce it. Buttresses are fairly common in Romanesque and Early English Gothic architecture and provide support to act against the sideways forces caused by the weight of the roof structures. In Decorated Gothic architecture the flying buttress was favoured.

Glossary of terms

Capital

A capital is the top of a column shaped to broaden the area of the column to bear the load thrusting down upon it. Neo-classical capitals are usually one of three Greek Orders: See Classical Orders.

Causewayed enclosure

A circular flat area surrounded by ditches with multiple entrances or causeways. These Neolithic earthworks were probably used for feasting and trade and perhaps had a funereal purpose.

Celts

The Celts were not a single ethnic group but rather the inhabitants of Iron Age Europe who shared a language, cultural traits and art forms inspired by the La Tene culture.

Chancel

The east part of a church, usually reserved for the clergy, where the high altar is normally located.

Glossary of terms

Chantry chapel

A small chapel used for prayers. In Pre-Reformation England is was common for the wealthy to fund such chapels so that priests would pray for them and thus speed the passage of their souls through Purgatory to Heaven.

Choir

That part of the church, usually part of the chancel, used by the singers.

Classical Orders

These are the rules that governed the design of buildings of Ancient Greece and Rome including the size and shape of columns, the ornamentation of the capitals and the design of the entablature. The three main orders — the Doric, Ionic, and Corinthian— originated in Greece. To these the Romans added the Tuscan, which they made simpler than the Doric, and the Composite, which combined the Ionic and the Corinthian.

Clerestory

A row of high-level windows to lighten the nave, a common feature of Gothic architecture.

Coade stone

An artificial weatherproof stone invented by Eleanor Coade. A paste was made of white clay, crushed stone and sand which was moulded and then fired. It was very popular for moulding Neo-classical statues (such as the Caryatids at St. Pancras New Church) and architectural decorations.

Coffer

A series of sunken panels in a ceiling or vault in the shape of a square, rectangle, or octagon. Usually coffers were moulded in plaster but they were sometimes painted illusions. The illustration is of the ceiling of the Cupola Room in Kensington Place, where they are a mixture of the two.

Colonnade

A long sequence of columns joined by their entablature, often free-standing, or sometimes part of a building. An example is to the side of the Queen's House in Greenwich.

Composite Order

The Composite Order is a mixed Order, combining the scrolls (volutes) of an Ionic Order capital with the acanthus leaves of the Corinthian Order.

Corbel

A structural piece of stone jutting from a wall (a type of bracket) designed to carry a weight such as of a balustrade or hammer-beam roof. Also, as shown in the illustrated corbel from Southwark Cathedral, they were often used in Gothic architecture to provide support for roof vaulting.

Glossary of terms

Corinthian Order

The Corinthian Order is the most ornate of the Greek Orders, characterized by a slender fluted column having an ornate capital often decorated with acanthus leaves. The length of the column is ten times its diameter and the column has 24 flutes.

Cornice

From the Italian meaning 'ledge', a cornice is a horizontal decorative moulding, usually the topmost component of an entablature.

Crocket

A hook-shaped decorative element projecting from the sloping angles of pinnacles and spires. The name derives from the French 'croc' meaning 'hook'.

Crossing

The part of a cruciform (in the shape of a cross) church where the four arms of the chancel, nave and the two transepts meet.

Glossary of terms

Crypt

An underground room or vault beneath a church used as a chapel or burial place. A purely secular underground room is known as an undercroft.

Cupola

A small, most often dome-like, structure on top of a building to admit light and air. The illustration is of a cupola on the National Gallery.

Cusping

Small decorative points projecting from the curve of an arch in Decorated Gothic architecture. The cusps might themselves have cusps for even greater elaboration.

Dome

A spherical vault resting on a circular base wall.

Doric Order

The Doric Order is the simplest of the Greek Orders, characterised by short heavy columns with a height that is only six times their diameter and with 20 flutes. The plain, round capitals have a convex echinus and a square abacus.

Dutch gable

The sides of a Dutch (or Flemish) gable have one or more curves. The gable may be an entirely decorative projection above a flat section of roof line, or may be the termination of a roof. The Dutch gable was a feature of the Renaissance architecture which spread from the Low Countries, arriving in Britain at the end of the sixteenth century. The illustration is of Holland House.

Entablature

An entablature is the superstructure of mouldings and bands which lies horizontally above columns, resting on their capitals. They are commonly divided into the lowest (architrave), the middle (frieze), and the highest (cornice).

Glossary of terms

Fan vaulting

A feature of Perpendicular Gothic architecture, this most complicated of vaults involves multiple ribs grouped in the shape of an open fan. Examples in London are in the Henry VII Chapel in Westminster Abbey and, as illustrated, the undercroft of Lincoln's Inn Chapel. Sometimes, as at Lincoln's Inn Chapel, there are short ribs connecting the main ribs, this is known as Lierne vaulting.

Flying buttress

A stone structure that helps to transfer the load of the roof to a detached pier or buttress through a half-arch or 'flying' buttress. The best examples in London can be seen at Westminster Abbey and, as illustrated, at Southwark Cathedral. St. Paul's Cathedral has flying buttresses but they are not visible as they are hidden by the outer walls.

Friars

Friars took vows of poverty, chastity and obedience and worked among the community supported by donations. Black Friars (Dominicans), Grey Friars (Franciscans), White Friars (Carmelites) and Austin Friars

(Augustinians) all had large precincts within London's city walls.

Frieze

Extensively used in Classical architecture a frieze is a decorative horizontal band, usually the central component of an entablature. This example of a simple Greek frieze is from Sir John Soane's house in Lincoln's Inn Fields. The Athenaeum in Waterloo Place has a much more flamboyant one.

Gallery

An upper story of a building open to the interior or exterior. Wooden internal galleries were a common feature of Wren Baroque churches.

Groin vaulting

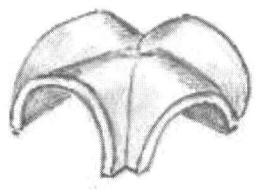

A groin vault is a feature of Romanesque architecture produced by the intersection, at right angles, of two barrel vaults. The word 'groin' refers to the elliptical edge between the intersecting vaults. A good example is in the Pyx Chamber in Westminster Abbey.

Hammer-beam roof

A hammer-beam roof is a feature of late Gothic English architecture. Short beams project from the wall (the hammer-beams) that support upward beams (the hammer-posts). Extra support is provided by curved arch braces resting on corbels which distribute the weight of the roof. Good examples are at Middle Hall Temple, Lambeth Palace and Eltham Palace with the largest being in Westminster Hall in the Palace of Westminster.

Ionic Order

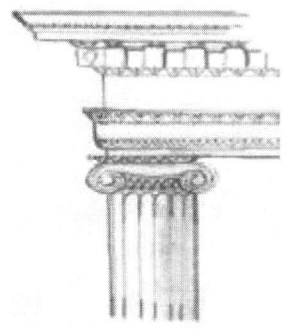

The Ionic Order is distinguished by slender, fluted pillars with a large base and two opposed scrolls (also called volutes) in the capital. The height of a column of the Ionic Order is nine times its lower diameter and the column has 24 flutes. The architrave of the entablature commonly consists of three stepped bands.

Lancet

A tall narrow pointed Early Gothic window with no tracery. This example is from the retrochoir at Southwark Cathedral.

Lantern light

A method of introducing light into buildings. The illustrated example is from the top of the Great Hall at Lambeth Palace.

La Tene Style

The style of Celtic art that had spread through most of Europe by the fifth century BC. It is characterised by curvilinear designs based mainly on vegetable and foliage motifs such as vines, tendrils and lotus flowers. It is found on luxury metalwork items such as the illustrated Wandsworth Shield.

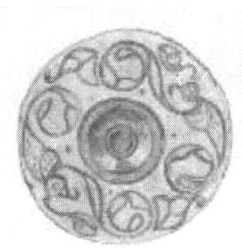

Glossary of terms

Long barrow

Early Neolithic burial mounds first appearing around 4500 BC. The barrow, was made up of soil excavated from ditches dug along the sides.

Mullion

An element of tracery, a mullion is a vertical bar dividing glass panes in a window.

Nave

The west part of a church where most of the congregation sit.

Niche

An ornamental recess often curved at the back and top and often containing a statue. This example is a niche in the Victorian Temple Bar in Fleet Street (as opposed to the Stuart Temple Bar that has been relocated to Paternoster Square).

Ogee arches

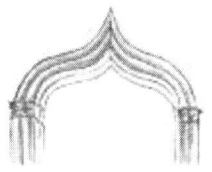

An arch shaped with two curves each side, one convex and the other concave. This was an important feature of Decorated Gothic architecture as it enabled the creation of sinuous curves and interlocking patterns.

Oriel window

This projecting, multi-sided window became popular in the Tudor period. Cantilevered from an upper floor, an Oriel window is supported from beneath by a bracket or corbel. The illustrated example is from inside the Church of St. Bartholomew-the-Great.

Palladian window

Also known as a 'Venetian window', the central round arched opening is flanked by a pair of smaller straight windows with columns and entablatures. This style of window can be seen in Burlington House or, as illustrated, at Horse Guards.

Panelling

A decorative pattern applied to the surface of stone or wood.

Pediment

A gable, usually of a triangular shape, above a horizontal structure. A pediment is an important element of a portico such as at the Royal Exchange. Pediments were also used to decorate the space above windows and doors. In Neo-classical architecture these are often 'broken' (where the cornice is left open at the apex) or 'open' (where there is a gap along the base). A variant of the broken pediment is the 'Swan-necked' pediment as illustrated above a door at Chartered Accountants' Hall.

Pendant

An elongated boss at the centre of a fan vault. A feature of the late Perpendicular Gothic period.

Pier

A rectangular column

Pilaster

A flat column or pier usually with a capital and base, attached to a wall. Pilasters give the impression of providing structural support but are only for decoration.

Pinnacle

A small turret or spire often on the top of a buttress. By extending the buttress upwards, pinnacles add weight.

Portico

A portico is a porch leading to the entrance of a building. Porticos are a common feature of Classical and Neo-classical architecture. A fine example is the illustrated entrance to the Royal Exchange.

Reredos

A wooden or stone structure standing behind the altar, usually decorated with quotations from the bible and often with paintings or sculptures. Wooden reredoses were a common feature of Wren churches and some, such as the illustrated example from St. Margaret's, Lothbury, were carved by Grinling Gibbons.

Retrochoir

The area behind the choir.

Rib vaulting

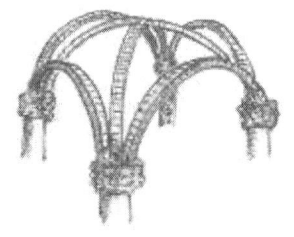

Rib (or ribbed) vaulting is where the inner vault surface is subdivided by a number of independent supporting arches, or ribs. The ribs are structurally independent from the surface behind them. The most common form is quadripartite rib vaulting where a vault is formed between four columns in a square and each column is joined to the three other by an arch or rib.

Rococo

A later, more elaborate, version of Baroque architecture. It was less symmetrical and used numerous curves and decorations often depicting jocular

163

themes. While very popular in Continental Europe it was considered rather frivolous for British taste. Other than a large rotunda in the Ranelagh Gardens there was little built in London in this style although it influenced the work of the Adam brothers in the late eighteenth century.

Rood screen

A screen, often elaborately carved, dividing the nave from the chancel. Rood screens sometimes included latticework which made it possible to partially see into the chancel from the nave. Most rood screens were removed during the Reformation but some were reinstated by the Victorians.

Rose window

A circular window sometimes known as a 'wheel window' where the window panes are divided into segments by stone mullions and tracery. There are good examples in the transepts at Westminster Abbey and, as illustrated, in St. Katherine Cree which is thought to modelled on the rose window in 'Old' St. Paul's.

Rustication

Blocks of masonry with roughened surfaces, separated by deep joints. Often used at the base of a building to give the impression of strength as here at Horse Guards.

Sanctuary

The east end of the chancel where the high altar is located.

Scagliora

A form of low cost artificial marble that came into fashion in seventeenth-century Tuscany. Made from stone fragments, Plaster of Paris, pigments and glue, scagliora was used for the Corinthian columns at each end of the chapel in the Royal Hospital for Seamen, Greenwich.

Spandrel

The decorated triangular space between arches. Also, the space between a rectangular door frame and the top of a door arch or, as here, the triangular shape above the niche containing the memorial to William Shakespeare in Southwark Cathedral.

Spire

A steeply pointed pyramidal or conical termination to a tower.

Steeple

A tall tower topped by a spire and often incorporating a belfry, as illustrated in Wren's St. Bride's Church.

Stucco

A fine plaster used for coating wall surfaces or for moulding plaster into architectural decorations. It is applied wet and dries into a very hard solid.

Tester

A canopy over the pulpit that acts as a sounding board. Pictured is the tester and pulpit, designed by William Newman, in St. Stephen's Walbrook.

Tracery

The stonework supporting the glass in a window. There are two main types. The earlier form is known as plate tracery because the glazed openings in the window have the appearance of being cut out of a flat plate of masonry. The later, bar tracery (as illustrated), uses narrow stone mullions, fitted together with mortar and metal pins, to form patterns.

Transept

A lateral part of a church extending to the north and south of the crossing.

Trefoil

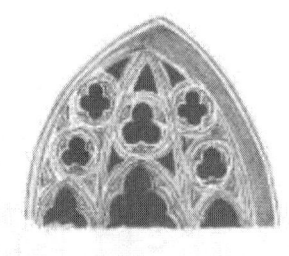

A shape formed from three partially overlapping circles used in some Gothic windows, tracery and panelling. In Christianity, a trefoil shape symbolises the Holy Trinity. The fourfold version of a trefoil is a quatrefoil. Trefoils and quatrefoils can be combined as illustrated in the Neo-gothic tracery in All Saints Church, Margaret Street.

Tympanum

The area inside a pediment, often used for sculpture.

Undercroft

An underground storage room, its secular function differs from that of a crypt.

Votive offering

Objects deposited in a sacred place for broadly religious purposes. They were generally made in order to gain favour with supernatural forces.

Window heads

The space above the top of the lancets.

Bibliography

Ackroyd, Peter	London, The Biography
Black, Jeremy	London
Cragoe, Carol	How to Read Buildings
English Heritage	Website http://www.english-heritage.org.uk
Gray, Robert	A History of London
Humphrey, Stephen	London's Churches and Cathedrals
Jenkins, Simon	England's Thousand Best Churches
Museum of London	London Sugar and Slavery
National Trust	Website http://www.nationaltrust.org.uk
Oliver, Neil	The History of Ancient Britain
Rice, Matthew	Rice's Architectural Primer
Rogers, Chris	How to Read London
Ross and Clark	London: The illustrated History
Starkey, David	Crown & Country
Thurley, Simon	The Building of England
Tucker, Tony	City of London Churches
Watkin, David	English Architecture
Williams, Brenda	The Romans in Britain
Winn, Christopher	I Never Knew That About London

Detailed notes

Pre-history

[1] The **Dagenham idol** is an early Bronze Age wooden statue of a naked human figure. Dating to around 2250 BC, it has two legs but no arms and a rounded head. A hole in the pubic region can be interpreted as indicating a female or, if a peg had been inserted, a male. The statue was found in 1922 in marshland on the north bank of the Thames in Dagenham. The original statue is on loan to the Valence House Museum in Dagenham with a copy in the Museum of London.

[2] Today the Thames' **tidal head** is far to the west at Teddington. The tidal head has changed throughout history largely in response to changes in sea level. Later it was influenced by the width of the river and, in particular, the wharves and flood defences that were built. The evidence of algae sensitive to changes in water salinity suggests the river's tidal head lay upstream of Westminster in the Bronze Age and by the Roman period it had receded to a point just to the east of London Bridge. This suggests that sea levels fell over this period which, while possibly the result of isostatic uplift, seems counter-intuitive.

[3] The heavily fortified site at **Woolwich Arsenal** (now largely covered by the Woolwich Power Station) dates from 250 BC. It is possible that the massive ditches that surround it were designed to keep people in rather than out and that Woolwich was a holding area for slaves awaiting export to the Continent, perhaps to the expanding Roman Empire.

Roman London

⁴ Much of the area on the south bank of the Thames was marshy although there was a narrow strip of gravel close to London Bridge which likely influenced the routes of the **Roman roads** approaching from the south. Most of the important Roman roads are aligned with London Bridge. The exception is Watling Street which appears to cross the river at Westminster where there may have been a pre-existing Celtic ford.

⁵ Remains of a **Roman bath** complex have been found on Huggin Hill, just to the south of Queen Victoria Street. A section of the retaining wall of the bath house survives in Cleary Gardens. Other Roman bath remains have been found in the basement of the office block at 101 Lower Thames Street (this site is periodically open to the public).

⁶ Two new gates in the **city walls** were added later. Aldersgate (between Newgate and Cripplegate) was added in the Roman period around 350 and Moorgate (between Cripplegate and Bishopsgate) was built in 1415 in order to give access to the newly drained Moorfields.

⁷ The **riverside wall** was less well built and may have been constructed in a rush. Traditional thinking is that the extension of the wall along the Thames was designed to thwart Saxon raiders. However, it is also possible that the river wall may be linked to the events of 285 when Carausius, with the support of Londinium, assumed the title of Emperor of Britain. Carausius was strong enough to withstand counter-moves for seven years and the wall may have been built for this purpose. In any event it took another three years before Emperor Constantius Chlorus was able to retake the country and Londinium may have been punished for its support of the rebellion.

---

[8] The location of Londinium's first **Christian cathedral** is uncertain. Legend links it to the site of the present church of St. Peter-upon-Cornhill (designed by Wren following the Great Fire). However, in 1995, a large ornate fourth century building was discovered on Tower Hill which may have been the cathedral.

Early Medieval London

[9] The **term 'Saxon'** is over-simplistic. In reality, a number of Germanic nations settled in different parts of Britain. Jutes from Jutland settled in Kent and the Isle of Wight; Saxons and Frisians from the Lower Rhine settled in the South of England and Angles from Schleswig-Holstein occupied East Anglia, the Midlands and the North of England.

[10] It is possible that the extent to which **Londinium was abandoned** after the Romans left has been overstated. Some believe that the east of the city remained a Romano-British stronghold for many years and that, over time, the Saxons inhabited the western part around Ludgate Hill. Support for this theory comes from the existence of two sets of wharves (Queenhithe and Billingsgate) and two markets (West Cheap and East Cheap). The location of churches also suggests that there was occupation within the walls long before Alfred created his burgh in 886. As early as 604 Æthelberht of Kent built the first St. Paul's Cathedral on Ludgate Hill and references to St Alban's Wood Street go back to 793.

[11] Evidence of a southern abutment of a **wooden bridge** built between 980 and 1000 was discovered on the Southwark shore in 1984. London was subsequently captured by the Vikings and it is thought that in 1014 the Saxon king Ethelred used his ships to pull this bridge down and that this action gave rise to the nursery rhyme 'London Bridge is Falling Down'. It is perhaps more likely that this nursery rhyme was inspired by the poor condition of the bridge for much of the later Middle Ages.

---

[12] The **derivation of the name London** from Londinium is fairly obvious. During the Norman period the area within the old Roman walls started to be referred to as Lundin, Londoun, Lunden or Londen. Over the centuries, the spelling settled down on London. Some believe that the name for the Roman settlement, Londinium, was derived from the Celtic word Plowonida which was thought to mean 'river that is difficult to cross'. Given its width and strong tidal flows the description of the river is more understandable than the etymology!

[13] These **Norman castles** belonged to powerful Norman nobles and were destroyed in 1213 after the nobles were involved in a rebellion. Both sites were given to Dominican Black Friars and the area is today known as 'Blackfriars'.

[14] Originally the **City of London's administrative system** involved 24 wards; there are now 25 wards as Farringdon ward was split in two in 1394. Each ward was headed by an Alderman who was selected from noblemen and wealthy merchants. In the Late Medieval period the dominance of this elite group was challenged by wealthy artisan workers, eager to gain power.

Late Medieval London

[15] The City of London played an active role in the events that led to the signing of **Magna Carta** in 1215 and the Mayor of London was appointed, along with the barons, to see that its provisions were carried out. London was the only city specifically named in the document, in the clause that stated that 'the City of London shall have all its ancient liberties by land as well as by water.' Magna Carta required London's mayors to be presented to the sovereign for approval and to take an oath to be faithful. These provisions have been respected ever since, and still govern the annual election and swearing in of the Lord Mayor. The City of London's 1297 version of Magna Carta, on view at Guildhall Art Gallery, includes Edward I's seal and the original writ ordering that the Charter be promulgated within the City.

Detailed notes

---

[16] As ships got larger the need for deeper water access to the shore increased and **wooden wharves** were built out into the river. The wood rotted fairly quickly and, rather than replacing the rotten timbers, it was easier to build new revetments in front of the old and fill in the space behind with soil and rubbish. Stone wharves were first built around 1400 and gradually the waterfront ceased advancing into the river. By the end of the Middle Ages the current riverfront between Blackfriars and the Tower of London had been largely established.

[17] The Steelyard (located on the waterfront immediately to the east of the Walbrook River) was the London base for the **Hanse merchants** from Cologne and Lubeck. This and the neighbouring Vintry (where French wine importers were based) were the largest enclaves of foreigners in Medieval London. London suffered periodic bouts of xenophobia and French and Italian merchants and Jews were periodically attacked, especially at the time of the Peasants' Revolt. People from Flanders, Holland and Zeeland (collectively 'the Dutch') settled in Southwark where they made clothing, pottery and beer (adding hops to the brew for the first time).

[18] **Cheapside** was the site of the principal produce markets in London with the word 'cheap' meaning 'market'. Many of the streets feeding into the main thoroughfare are named after the produce that was once sold, including Honey Lane, Milk Street, Bread Street, Wood Street and Poultry. Gutter Lane might also be a reference to butchery although most of this took place just outside the walls at nearby Smithfield.

[19] In 1515, the Court of Aldermen of the City of London settled an order of precedence for the 48 **Livery Companies** then in existence, which was based on their relative economic and political power. The first 12 Livery Companies are known as the 'Great Twelve' with the top three being the Mercers, Grocers and Drapers. The Merchant Taylors and the Skinners have always disputed their precedence, so once a year they exchange sixth and seventh place hence the phrase 'being at sixes and sevens'.

Detailed notes

[20] Between 1092 and 1814 the Thames froze in London at least 24 times although the ice was not always thick or flat enough for a **Frost Fair** to be held. 1683/84 was the coldest winter on record and a fair was held on the ice for ten weeks. Food and entertainment such as skittles and bull baiting took place and tents were erected for selling mementos. The river has not frozen in Central London since the medieval London Bridge was replaced in 1831.

[21] The work of Italian craftsmen, the **shrine to Edward the Confessor** with its stone base and canopy, was originally encrusted with gold mosaic and inlaid with precious marbles. In its base there were six niches for pilgrims to kneel in. This symbol of Catholicism was dismantled during the Dissolution of the Monasteries. It was reinstated under Queen Mary but when the shrine was reassembled various parts were placed upside-down. Although some damage has been done, and the reliquary chest lost, it is remarkable that the shrine has survived the widespread destruction of religious icons that took place during the Reformation.

[22] The **Knights Templar**, whose original purpose was protecting pilgrims visiting the Holy Land, became too wealthy and powerful for their own good and were attacked by the authorities in Spain and France. Under pressure from the Pope, in 1307 Edward II banished the Templars and passed much of their London property to the Knights of St. John who, in turn, leased it to lawyers. The Templar movement was finally disbanded by the Pope in 1312.

[23] **London's walls** were strengthened in the Middle Ages. Between 1211 and 1213 a new defensive ditch was dug around the outside and towers such as those at St. Giles Cripplegate were added. The postern gate by the Tower of London was constructed between 1297 and 1308 to improve security at the eastern end of the wall and to provide access for pedestrians. Around 1415 a new gate, Moorgate, was built between Cripplegate and Bishopsgate. London Wall was to remain until the eighteenth century when demolition of parts of it commenced. Most of it was gone by the mid-nineteenth century.

---

[24] Those who survived the **Black Death** faced very changed economic and social conditions. There was a shortage of skilled labour and land owners changed from arable farming to sheep farming which required less manpower. Hungry peasants left the land and moved to the cities. While those in work benefitted from a rise in wages, churchmen complained of a collapse in morals and a breakdown in respect for the church and the law.

[25] **John of Gaunt** was especially unpopular. A son of Edward III, he was Regent to the infant Richard II and in 1380 introduced a poll tax that required each man over the age of 15 to pay a shilling. This was one of the direct causes of the Peasants' Revolt.

[26] During the **Wars of the Roses**, the Yorkists won an important victory at Barnet in 1471. Soon after this, William Neville tried to lead an army of 17,000 Lancastrian supporters through London. Permission was refused, and after a short siege and after having burnt the eastern suburbs, Neville's men were forced back by the militia. However, Londoners had been scared and the city walls underwent substantial restoration and improvement.

Tudor London

[27] The changes in agricultural practices that followed the Black Death continued into the Tudor period. In rural England there was a significant rise in **land enclosure**. Enclosures, which were often undertaken unilaterally by the landowner, usually resulted in a loss of common land and peasant rights. The consequential hardships accelerated rural depopulation.

[28] In his early years Henry VIII was a sincere Roman Catholic and indeed authored a book strongly criticising Martin Luther and the Northern European **Reformation movement**. Despite the reluctance of his Chancellors Cardinal Wolsey and Thomas More, Henry found it expedient, and indeed very profitable, to separate the Church of England from the Pope and Rome. While the Act of Supremacy nominally made the country Protestant, strong support

for Rome remained for well over a century and there was a very real risk that Catholicism would be reinstated. Gradually a middle way between the Roman Catholic and European Protestant traditions developed. In services the emphasis changed from the Holy Communion to the preaching of sermons. As a result the pulpit, rather than the chancel, became the point of focus within churches and rood screens were removed.

29 Built in 1501, **Richmond Palace** was a favourite home of Elizabeth I, who died there in 1603. It remained a royal residence until the death of Charles I in 1649 but within months of his execution the palace was sold by order of Parliament. Over the following ten years it was demolished and the only surviving traces are the Wardrobe and the Gate House. The fine porticoed Trumpeters' House was built between 1736 and 1756.

30 Humphrey, Henry VI's Regent, built **Greenwich Palace** in 1433. Henry VII rebuilt the palace between 1498 and 1504 based around three large courtyards. It was the birthplace of King Henry VIII and featured prominently in his life. Both Queens Mary and Elizabeth lived there for some years during the sixteenth century. During the reign of James I the Queen's House was erected to the south and the palace was allowed to fall into disrepair. In 1660, Charles II decided to rebuild the palace but the only section to be completed was part of the present King Charles Court. Most of the rest of the palace was demolished, and the site remained empty until construction of the Royal Hospital for Seamen began in 1694.

31 Perhaps the largest investment in Tudor palaces was made in **Nonsuch Park** near Ewell in Surrey which was used for hunting parties from 1538. While the spectacular palace incorporated some of the stone work from the dissolved Merton Priory its design was a first step towards Classical architecture. The palace was demolished in 1683 and there is little to be seen in Ewell today. Some stucco panels from Nonsuch Palace are however on display in the Museum of London.

Stuart London

[32] The limited supply of **clean water** was a factor inhibiting London's growth. The situation was improved in 1613 with the opening of the New River. This was a 39-mile artificial waterway that took drinking water from the River Lea and nearby streams into Clerkenwell.

[33] The **Puritans** were an extreme form of Protestant who were critical of the religious compromises made during Elizabeth I's reign. They encouraged direct personal religious experience, sincere moral conduct and simple worship services. Such thinking appealed to the poor as it gave them hope that virtue and self-discipline would be rewarded. Puritan leaders asked James I for reforms including the abolition of bishops but the king rejected most of their proposals. In the years that followed the Crown and the church hierarchy, especially under Archbishop William Laud, repressed the Puritans causing many to emigrate to America.

[34] In 1611 James I **suspended Parliament** and it did not meet again until 1621 when James recalled Parliament to discuss the future marriage of his son, Charles, to a Catholic Spanish princess. The largely Protestant Parliament was outraged and, although the marriage never took place, this further damaged relationships. Charles I, like a number of short men, was both arrogant and stubborn and between 1625 and 1629 there were many disputes over money and religion. In 1629 Charles refused to let Parliament meet and ruled by using his Court of the Star Chamber. After the Scots invaded England in 1639 Charles was forced to recall Parliament as only they could provide the necessary funds to fight a war.

[35] There was very little fighting at the 'battle' of **Turnham Green.** Although the Royalist army was outnumbered and short of ammunition, it would probably have made light work of the London militia. However, needing the future support of London, Charles I was advised that a slaughter of these poorly armed civilians would further alienate the city.

---

36 The eleven miles of **defensive earthworks** around London were constructed to a Dutch military design. Building them was a massive effort that involved 100,000 men, women and children. The extent to which the Royalists were feared is shown by the fact that Puritan preachers encouraged them to work on Sundays. The area enclosed by the earthworks was much larger than the medieval walls. It included Westminster, Covent Garden and Aldgate as well as an area to the south of the river.

37 **Oliver Cromwell,** a devout Puritan, had been Member of Parliament for Huntington before the Civil War and, during it, second in command of the New Model Army. He was one of the signatories of King Charles I's death warrant in 1649, and he dominated the short-lived Commonwealth of England. He was a prominent member of the Rump Parliament and commanded the bloody campaign in Ireland in 1649. In 1653, he set up a short-lived assembly, known as the Barebone's Parliament, before being invited by his fellow leaders to rule as Lord Protector of England. He died from natural causes in 1658 and was buried in Westminster Abbey. However, after the Restoration his corpse was dug up, hung in chains, and beheaded!

38 The **Navigation Acts** first enacted by Cromwell's Rump Parliament in 1651, were a series of laws that prohibited Britain's colonies from trading directly with the Netherlands, Spain, France, and their colonies. This policy, known as mercantilism, was designed to maximise Britain's wealth and remained for nearly 200 years.

39 The **Great Fire** started in Pudding Lane (close to London Bridge) in the early hours of 2 September 1666. Fanned by strong easterly winds it raged for four days destroying most of the houses within the city walls. Although it is now   thought to have started by accident in a bakery there were suspicions that it was started as part of a Catholic plot to prepare the way for a French invasion. The efforts of the Lord Mayor proved ineffective in the first two days and King Charles II and his brother James personally took charge of fighting the fire. However, the techniques available were inadequate and the use of gunpowder to blow up houses to create a fire wall, while saving the

Tower of London, was used too late. Most people lost everything they owned and had to live in makeshift tents and sheds in fields in Islington, Moorfields and Highgate. Some people lived like this for up to eight years. Some 436 acres of the city were destroyed and in total 13,000 houses, 44 livery halls and 87 churches were lost as well as important buildings such as St. Paul's Cathedral and the Royal Exchange. Only ten people were recorded as having been killed by the fire but it caused a great deal of hardship and financial suffering as houses were not insured. The fire did not spread south of the river (or indeed damage London Bridge which was saved by a fire break resulting from an earlier fire) but Southwark was to have its own 'Great Fire' in 1676.

40 **Planning controls** were used to replace wooden houses with brick built ones to lessen the risk of future fires and four different types of house (each related to particular street width) were mandated. A special court was set up to determine whether the landlord or the tenant were responsible for the reconstruction. Generally, where the landlord lacked the funds the tenant was encouraged to pay for the work with the length of the lease being extended and rent reduced in compensation. If the property was not rebuilt within three years there were provisions for compulsory purchase. Examples of the new properties can be seen today at Amen Corner and Kings Bench Walk (both in EC4) but few of the newly rebuilt houses survived the Second World War. Livery Halls fared better and the rebuilt Apothecaries', Vintners' and Skinners' Livery Halls have all survived.

41 Three building innovations helped **property development** after the Great Fire. The production of some building materials was industrialised with the standardisation of bricks and the prefabrication of windows, doors and cornices. The City authorities relaxed the restrictions imposed by the medieval guilds and, for the first time, non-freemen were able to work in the City. Most importantly a system of contracts, leases and mortgages encouraged speculators such as Nicholas Barbon. The business model for financing the new property developments had been established when

Detailed notes

Bloomsbury Square was built in 1661. This involved the Earl of Southampton dividing his land into plots that were let to developers for 42-year terms at low rents on the condition that houses were built to a prescribed style. This had the advantage to the landowner of limiting the capital needed to invest while allowing him to control the style of the development and to share in the ultimate profits. It offered the developer the opportunity of large short-term profits when they sold the leases on the new houses.

[42] Protestant **Huguenots** had been coming to London to avoid persecution in Catholic Europe for many years. Between 1550 and 1585, for example, it is estimated that 40,000 emigrated to the city from the Netherlands. Others came from France and this turned into a flood when the Edict of Nantes was revoked by Louis XIV in 1685. Up to 80,000 French Huguenots are thought to have come to England in the next few years with many settling in London. Around 1690 it is estimated that French Huguenots amounted to about eight percent of London's population with many living in the Spitalfields area.

[43] The origins of English banking date back to the London goldsmiths. The goldsmiths developed the basic banking practices of accepting deposits on which interest was paid, making loans from such deposits, issuing their own promissory notes (or banknotes) and allowing depositors to access their accounts by use of 'drawn notes' (or cheques). Their activities were to be constrained, however, by the founding of the **Bank of England** in 1694. Modelled on the Bank of Amsterdam, as well as managing the national debt, the Bank of England became the most powerful financial institution in the land by facilitating transactions and dispensing credit to merchants and entrepreneurs. In 1708 the Bank of England was granted a monopoly of joint stock banking and other banks were prohibited from having more than six partners. This provision effectively shaped the development of English banking until 1826, when the legislation was repealed and joint stock banks were again permitted and private banks grew (see note 73). The Bank of England first operated from Mercers Hall. A purpose-built building was constructed in 1734 which was extended and then rebuilt by Sir John Soane between 1788 and 1830.

181

---

[44] The **South Sea Company** was founded in 1711 as a public-private partnership to reduce the cost of the national debt. In the Treaty of Utrecht Britain was granted a monopoly to sell slaves to South America and this right was assigned to the company. The value of the company's stock rose rapidly as it rapidly expanded its operations. However, political problems and the renewal of war with Spain meant that the business was not as profitable as expected. In 1720 the value of the company's shares collapsed and the financial crisis that resulted became known as the 'South Sea Bubble'. Legislation followed that required new companies to have a Royal Charter or be approved by an Act of Parliament. This 'Bubble Act' greatly reduced the number of new companies being formed for the next century. Its repeal in 1825 paved the way for the expansion of corporate activity in the Victorian period.

[45] Prohibition of alcohol during the Commonwealth led to a massive increase in the drinking of tea and coffee. The first **coffee house**, which opened in 1652, was in St. Michael's Alley, Cornhill and is now the Jamaica Wine House. By 1663 there were 82 coffee houses in London and by 1739 there were 551. Londoners liked their coffee sweet and this led to the increase in demand for sugar. This was a catalyst for expanded production in the West Indies and the growth in the slave trade

[46] **Inigo Jones** (1573 –1652) had toured Italy extensively and was the first English architect to incorporate the Classical Orders in his buildings with their rules of proportion and symmetry. He was a favourite of the Stuart kings and his main works were the Queen's House in Greenwich, the Banqueting House in Whitehall, Covent Garden (although only St. Paul's Church remains) and the Queen's Chapel in St. James' Palace. He added a large portico to the 'Old' St. Paul's and is even thought to be responsible for the windows in the White Tower of the Tower of London.

Georgian London

[47] During the **Gordon Riots** the mob raged for six days. The 1780 riots were triggered by a debate in Parliament about whether to repeal the Catholic Relief Act. However, anti-Catholic sentiments may not have been the only motivation as the main targets seem to have been the prisons and the Bank of England. In all about 700 rioters died (mostly killed by the army) but no Catholics! The riots may have been a symptom of more widespread unrest. The anarchy of the French Revolution was just a few years later.

[48] **Carlton House** was a mansion on the south side of Pall Mall. From the 1780s it was the centre of a glittering alternate court to that of George III at St. James'. In 1820, on the death of his father, the Prince Regent became King George IV. He decided that Carlton House was inadequate for his lavish needs and decided to rebuild Buckingham House. Carlton House was demolished in 1825 and replaced with two massive white stuccoed terraces known as Carlton House Terrace.

[49] **Slavery** was well established before Britain became involved. However, it was the British that significantly increased the volume of the African slave trade and benefitted most from the profits it generated. Much of London's wealth in the Georgian period was derived, directly or indirectly, from the Caribbean plantations. These plantations needed slaves to operate profitably (European workers were more expensive and could not survive the climate). London played a central role in what became known as the 'Slave triangle'. Goods such as guns, textiles and manufactures goods were shipped to Africa to exchange for Africans negroes who were shipped to the Caribbean as slave labour for the plantations. Many died on the way. Sugar, rum, coffee and tobacco were brought back to England making massive profits for ship captains, plantation owners, merchants and financiers who funded and insured ships and cargoes. Between 1750 and 1779 London recorded 869 slave-trade sailings (the second largest number compared to 1,909 from Liverpool and 624 from Bristol). A number of prominent and wealthy

---

Anglicans had strong views about the need to abolish the slave trade. Initially, William Wilberforce and the Clapham Sect, and later Thomas Buxton, held rallies, printed pamphlets highlighting the horrors of slavery and petitioned Parliament. Despite growing support from non-conformist groups such as the Quakers and the Methodists, Wilberforce's first 1789 Anti-slavery Bill failed and legislation abolishing the trading of slaves in the British Empire was not passed until 1807. Legislation preventing the ownership of slaves had to wait until the Slavery Abolition Act of 1833.

[50] Robert Milligan, a merchant and ship owner, was largely responsible for the **West India Docks**. Two docks (the northern one for imports and the southern one for exports) were constructed between 1800 and 1802. Between them, the docks had a combined capability to berth over 600 vessels. Locks and basins at either end of the docks connected them to the Thames. The South West India Dock was constructed in the 1860s, replacing the unprofitable City Canal that had been built in 1805.

[51] Rivalry between London and Westminster was still intense and the City authorities were concerned that a **bridge at Westminster** would give competitive advantage to their neighbours. However, the migration of wealthy Londoners to the west created a new dynamic. Eventually, in 1736, Parliamentary support was obtained for a bridge at Westminster. The 15 arch bridge made from Portland stone was completed in 1750 and acted as a catalyst for housing and road improvements in Westminster. However, the new bridge did cause empty housing in the City and, in retaliation, approval was obtained in 1760 for building a new bridge at Blackfriars. The nine arch Portland stone bridge (originally called the William Pitt Bridge) opened in 1769 and led to economic regeneration especially in Southwark.

[52] While **newspapers** existed before the eighteenth century they only had small circulations. The Georgian period saw a great increase in circulation numbers and by 1801 London had 23 different newspapers. Many were printed in, or near to, Grub Street (now Milton Street in EC2) or around Fleet Street.

---

53 In 1728 Queen Caroline, a keen gardener, took almost 300 acres from Hyde Park to form **Kensington Gardens** and she separated the two parks with a long ditch or ha-ha. In Hyde Park a large lake, called the Serpentine, was made by damming the Westbourne Stream. The Serpentine was one of the first man-made lakes in England that was designed to look natural (previously artificial lakes were usually long and straight).

54 Gin, or 'Mother Geneva' as it was called, was a particular source of **drunkenness**. It was more available than fresh water and was consumed in quantity by men, women and even children. It is estimated that in 1723 the average per capita consumption was over a pint of gin per week. A licensing system was introduced in 1736 but it was largely ineffective and consumption remained high for the rest of the century.

55 John Wesley (1703-1791) and his brother Charles started the **Methodist movement** in 1738, initially as an offshoot of the Church of England. Their emphasis was on reaching out to the poor and providing spiritual and moral support as well as a degree of medical and educational assistance. Methodism was not encouraged either by the Church of England (which feared the return of Puritanism) or the authorities (who were worried about large groups of the poor gathering together). While John Wesley spent much of his time travelling and preaching he established a London base in a cannon foundry in 1739 and moved, just a few hundred yards up the road, to a new chapel in City Road in 1778. Interestingly, the new chapel was built on marsh land that had been filled with rubble from the 'Old' St. Paul's Cathedral that had been destroyed a century before in the Great Fire.

56 Six **Queen Anne Churches** were designed by Hawksmoor (including Christchurch Spitalfields, St. Luke's Old Street, St. Anne's Limehouse and St. Alfege's Greenwich). Other architects included John James (St. George's Hanover Square), James Gibbs (St. Martin-in-the-Fields) and Thomas Archer (St. John's Smith Square). While the Commissioners planned to build all the churches to the same design in practice there is considerable variety.

---

[57] William Kent's **Kew Palace**, known as the 'White House', was demolished in 1802 and George III commenced an expensive (and in the light of developments probably mad!) project to rebuild it as a Gothic castellated palace with multiple towers and turrets. The castle was never completed and was ultimately demolished. George III suffered periodic bouts of insanity and in 1810 his condition became permanent. In his later life, he suffered from deafness, blindness and dementia. During his periods of sickness, he moved his family to the much smaller building (the modern-day Kew Palace) which was called the 'nunnery' by his fun seeking unmarried daughters!

Regency London

[58] **Regent's Park**, previously known as Marylebone Park, was Crown land and the Prince Regent saw the financial potential in its development. John Nash's plan involved a small number of high value properties (including a palatial summer residence for George himself) surrounded by rural vistas. To boost the importance of this development it would be linked to Carlton House, then the centre of power, by a fine new road. In the event the summer palace and many of the aristocratic houses were not built. However, a lake and a zoo were created, the park was landscaped and around three sides fine terraced houses such as Clarence Terrace, Cornwall Terrace and York Terrace were constructed.

[59] Built of Cornish granite, **Waterloo Bridge** was opened by the Prince Regent in 1817, two years after the famous battle. Many considered this to be John Rennie's finest bridge and it features in a number of Claude Monet paintings. However, it was narrow and suffered from subsidence. In its wisdom, London County Council decided to demolish it in 1934 and replace it with a new concrete bridge. The new bridge was finally completed in 1945

[60] Designed by John Rennie and his son, the new five arched **London Bridge** took eight years to build. The project involved demolishing many houses to clear the way for approach roads. Rennie's bridge was replaced by the current crossing in 1973 and was sold to an American entrepreneur. It now stands in Lake Havasu City, Arizona.

---

61 The **Thames Tunnel** was built between 1825 and 1843 by Marc Isambard Brunel and his son Isambard Kingdom Brunel using the newly invented tunnelling shield (a movable wooden frame with 36 cells each holding a miner). The tunnel was originally intended for horse-drawn carriages but it was never used as, due to a lack of funding, access ramps were never built. Instead, for a few years, it became a popular attraction for sight-seeing pedestrians and later prostitutes. Interest in it faded and in 1865 it was purchased by the East London Railway Company.

62 Building the **St. Katherine Dock** necessitated the displacement of about 10,000 people and the demolition of a medieval hospital. Built by Thomas Telford the dock was used for tea, coffee, sugar, marble, ivory, rubber, wines and spirits. However, its use was short lived as it was too small and its narrow entrance could not admit larger steam-powered ships.

63 The Government considered the growth in agnosticism and non-conformist worship as a threat, especially following the French Revolution. This led to a programme of state-sponsored church building. These **Commissioners' Churches** were built as economically as possible with minimal ornamentation. The key objective was to seat as many people as possible. Designs were supervised by three Crown architects (John Nash, John Soane and Robert Smike) and a few of the churches were designed by them including Nash's All Souls, Langham Place. Other architects included George Gilbert Scott and Charles Barry.

64 In 1834 the **Palace of Westminster** was largely destroyed by fire. The blaze was caused by the burning of wooden tally sticks in the furnaces in the basement. The fire destroyed a large part of the palace, including St. Stephen's Chapel which at that time was the meeting place of the House of Commons. The actions of James Braidwood of the London Fire Engine Establishment, and a fortunate change in wind direction, meant that Westminster Hall survived. In 1836 a competition to design a new palace was won by Charles Barry. Barry's plans, developed in collaboration with Augustus Pugin, incorporated the surviving buildings into the new complex.

Victorian London

[65] The first **council estate** was not opened until 1890. Situated in Bethnal Green on the boundary with Shoreditch, the Boundary Estate, which is still in existence, consisted of multi-story brick tenements radiating from a central circus. A total of 1,069 tenements, mostly two or three-roomed flats, were planned in 23 blocks to accommodate 5,524 persons. Work was commenced by the Metropolitan Board of Works in 1893 and completed by the recently formed London County Council.

[66] Constructed in 1838, the **Euston Arch** was not really an 'arch' but rather a sandstone gateway consisting of a triangular pediment supported by four Doric columns. To the relief of the many who thought it ugly it was demolished in 1961 as part of the modernisation of the station.

[67] In 1846, a Royal Commission recommended the prohibition of further **railway lines from the north** entering the city. This explains the existence of four mainline stations along the Euston Road – from the west, Marylebone, Euston, St. Pancras and King's Cross. These stations were supported by a massive area of sidings and warehouses. An echo of them remains behind King's Cross in buildings such as the Granary, the Coal Drop and Ice Wharf that have now been attractively converted.

[68] The **first underground line**, the Metropolitan Railway, covered the four miles between Paddington and Farringdon Street using gas-lit wooden carriages hauled by steam, and therefore very smoky, locomotives. The line was laid in cuttings, mostly following existing streets. The cuttings were then covered with a continuous brick archway and the street replaced. Ventilation in the tunnels was a challenge and there were open air sections at regular intervals. In 1868 the first phase of what was to become the District Line opened from South Kensington to Westminster and in 1884 the Circle Line was completed. The first deep-level tube line was opened in 1890, with electric trains running from King William Street under the Thames to Stockwell (this is now part of the Northern Line).

---

⁶⁹ The first **horse drawn trams** appeared around 1870. Although tram lines were not laid in Central London for fear of increasing congestion, trams provided important links to the new suburbs especially in South West London. Trams were to revolutionised travel for the middle classes. They ran frequently to a timetable, were much cheaper than trains and were more comfortable than the omnibus.

⁷⁰ The **dock strike** began in August 1889 after a dispute about 'bonus' money during the unloading of a ship in the West India Docks. The strike soon spread to the other docks and lasted for about a month funded, in part, from donations from across the country and from Australia. The strike resulted in a victory for the 100,000 strikers who benefitted from a wage increase. However, working conditions were not improved and the infamous 'call-on' system continued until 1965.

⁷¹ The massive **Beckton Gas Works** was named after Simon Beck, the governor of the Gas Light and Coke Company. The 550 acre site in East Ham was chosen as it was possible to build deep water piers into the Thames enabling coal from the Durham coalfields to be easily unloaded. In 1949 Beckton was transferred to the North Thames Gas Board and it closed in 1969.

⁷² Initially **accountancy firms** mostly worked on insolvencies. However, changes in legislation led to a reduction in fees for liquidation work and an increase in those for audits. Initially audits were required for banks, insurance companies and railways but the 1900 Companies Act made audit a requirement for all registered companies.

⁷³ Legislation in 1826 allowed **banks** to limit their liability. This led to a period of growth and mergers between small private banks and regional banks were attracted to London. In 1833 the National Provincial Bank was established with a head office at Gibson Hall, 15 Bishopsgate. In 1884, Lloyds Bank (previously confined to the Midlands) took over two London banks and in 1891 Birmingham and Midland Bank (that became the Midland Bank before it was absorbed into HSBC) merged with the Central Bank of London Ltd.

Detailed notes

Barclays is older and traces its origins back to 1690 when John Freame, a Quaker, and Thomas Gould started trading as goldsmith bankers in Lombard Street. In 1736 Freame's son took on James Barclay as a partner. In 1896 the small family bank merged with 20 other small banks to form the joint stock bank Barclays and Co.

[74] In 1832 a group of fire insurance companies merged to form the London Fire Engine Establishment and James Braidwood was appointed its superintendent. This worked well until the massive **Tooley Street fire** of 1861 that burned for two days and destroyed six warehouses including Hay's Wharf. Braidwood died fighting the fire and there is a small memorial to him in Tooley Street. The size of the insurance claims related to the fire were so large that the insurance companies considered disbanding the fire service. The government intervened and passed responsibility to the Metropolitan Board of Works.

[75] The poor, weakened by terrible diets and working conditions, were especially vulnerable to **disease**. However, they did not have a vote and little was done about it until typhoid and cholera became prevalent amongst the wealthy. The link between cholera and polluted drinking water was not established until 1849 when Dr. John Snow published the results of his research. He confirmed his findings in 1855 when he traced the source of the 1853 epidemic to a public water pump in St. Giles. A replica of the pump is in Broadwick Street.

[76] Building Bazelgette's **Main Drainage System** was one of the largest civil engineering projects of the century involving the construction of five great sewers 82 miles in length. These took the sewage from pipes that previously drained directly into the Thames and transported it to new downstream works where it was released to be dispersed by tidal action. Gravity and steam pumping stations provided the power. Two pumping stations at Crossness and Abbey Mills (described as 'Cathedrals of Sewage') remain today. As part of this project the Victoria and Chelsea Embankments on the

---

north bank of the Thames and the Albert Embankment on the south bank were constructed. Designed to save lives, the new system was actually instrumental in the loss of about 600 lives in the Princess Alice disaster of 1878. This river accident happened close to the northern outfall of the sewage system at Barking and many of the dead were poisoned by raw sewage rather than drowned!

[77] An ever-expanding British Empire and increasing state involvement domestically meant that the number of civil servants more than doubled in Victoria's reign (64,000 in 1855 to 164,000 in 1895). New government departments were formed that were housed in fine new buildings in **Whitehall** designed to demonstrate the country's imperial power. These include the Foreign and Commonwealth Office in King Charles Street built in 1868 and designed by George Gilbert Scott. Building of another massive development, the New Government Offices on the corner of Whitehall and Parliament Square, commenced in 1898 and was finally completed in 1915.

[78] Organised by Henry Cole and other members of the RSA, and supported by Prince Albert, the **Great Exhibition** was to be a symbol of the Nation's leading role in technological progress. It contained over 100,000 exhibits, many from other countries, and attracted six million visitors over 140 days including many overseas tourists. It was located in Hyde Park, housed in a splendid glass, steel and wood 'palace' three times the length of St. Paul's Cathedral. The 'Crystal Palace' was designed by Joseph Paxton based on his designs for glasshouses at Chatsworth House. It contained over 294,000 panes of glass. After its six-month run the 'Crystal Palace' was moved to Penge Common, Sydenham where it was eventually destroyed by fire in 1936. Profits from the Exhibition were used to acquire land south of Hyde Park where the Albert Hall, the Museum of Science and Art (later called the Victoria and Albert Museum) and the Natural History Museum were built. The Science Museum was built in 1907.